Abbas Chalaby

ALL OF EGYPT

From Cairo to Abu Simbel and Sinai

2ND EDITION REVISED
In this edition have collaborated:
Giovanna Magi for the revision and integration of the text
Paolo Giambone for the photography

BONECHI

◀ *The god Osiris. (Valley of the Kings -*
Tomb of Sennedjen)

The monuments at Ghiza under the nighttime sky.

INTRODUCTION

THE ORIGINS

Egyptians history may have started in the paleolithic era even though that part of its history must consist entirely of hypotheses and suppositions. At that period the valley of the Nile was very different from what it is today. The river must have covered almost the whole region and this fact, together with a climate which was undoubtedly much more humid, would have resulted in unlimited expanses of marshland stretching right up to the Delta. The climate started to change at the end of the paleolithic period and this caused the Nile to change its course to that which it follows today. The slow but progressive change of the neighbouring areas into desert led to human life being concentrated along the fertile banks of the river. In the neolithic period whose beginning can be taken to be about 10,000 B.C., there were already two distinct ethnic groups originating from two very different regions. A group of African race from central Africa and a second group of Mediterranean race which had its origins in the heart of Asia. To these two must be added a third group, believed to come from the legendary Atlantis, which must have arrived in the Nile valley via Libya. Two centres of civilisation developed, one in the north of the country concentrated in the Delta where it created the first urban centre Merimda, the other in the south around Tasa.

Thus the Egyptian population was divided into two even at this remote period and not withstanding the subsequent unification of the country this has left its mark in the division into « hesep » or provinces which the Greeks called « nômi », Upper Egypt having 22 and Lower Egypt 20. This was the dawn of Egyptian civilisation, the period which the Egyptians themselves called the « time of God » when Osiris sat on the throne of Egypt. This terrestrial reign is described in documents known as *The Pyramid Texts*. Osiris, according to legend, united the two parts of the population but the unity did not last long. It is only from about 3200 B.C. that one can start to talk about Egyptian history in any serious sense.

Unity between Upper and Lower Egypt

The history starts with Narmer whom some scholars feel should be identified with the mythical king Menes who unified the two kingdoms. This is the beginning of the first of the thirty one dynasties which sat on the Egyptian throne until 332 B.C., the year that Egypt was conquered by Alexander the Great. « A breaker of heads he is... he does not spare » is what one can read in an ancient inscription about king Narmer. In fact this is how he is depicted on the famous « Narmer stele », a slate tablet about 74 centimetres high, dating from about 3100 B.C. and originating from Hierakonopolis (the ancient Nekneb, the present day El Kab), a city considered sacred in the prehistory of Upper Egypt. On this stele which had a cosmetic purpose, on one side we see the pharaoh with one hand grasping the hair of an enemy and the other a club. On this side of the stele the king wears the conical crown of Upper Egypt while on the other side he is depicted, in front of a large number of his decapitated enemies wearing the crown of Lower Egypt.

There were in fact three crowns: the White Crown of the North, the Red Crown of the South and the Double Crown, consisting of the two previous ones combined, which symbolised the united kingdom. Similarly the vulture was the symbol of Upper Egypt and the cobra that of Lower Egypt.

THE OLD KINGDOM

The Old Kingdom which had its beginnings round about 2700 B.C. is considered by many scholars to be the greatest period of the whole of Egyptian civilisation. It is also sometimes called the Memphis Kingdom, the capital being moved from Abydos to Memphis (Memphis, the capital of the 1st nôme of Lower Egypt). During this initial period of Egyptian history the first civil and religious laws, writing and artistic canons all came into existence. The first great Pharaoh was Zoser at the beginning of the third dynasty. He was responsible for the construction of the first of the great stone monuments of Egypt, the pyramid at Sakkarah. He also appointed a prime minister who assisted him with the royal administration which had become very extensive and complicated. Zoser also organised numerous military expeditions, for exemple to Nubia beyond the first cataract and to Sinai. The next dynasty, the IVth, started with Snefru who constructed a new type of pyramid, one with perfectly smooth faces. As far as architectonic magnificence is concerned however he was surpassed by three other pharaohs of the same dynasty: Cheops, Chefren, and Micernius the builders of the famous complex at Gizeh. Unfortunately we know very little about them

apart from the fact that Cheops organised a few military expeditions against Sinai. The fifth dynasty orginated in the city of Heliopolis and is therefore called the Heliopolitan dynasty because its first three pharaohs are said to have been conceived by the wife of a priest of Ra after intercourse with the god himself. From then on all pharaohs were called « sons of Ra » as a matter of course. It was during this period that the Pyramid Texts were composed and military expeditions against Asia and Libya carried out. The most important personality of the last dynasty of the Old Kingdom was Pepi II who succeeded to the throne at the age of six and remained there for ninety four years. His was the longest reign in Egyptian history. However at the end of the sixth dynasty the central government collapsed and power was divided up among the « nomarchs » or feudal princes who passed it from one to the other without the Pharaoh being able to intervene or oppose them in any way.

This gave rise to the *First Interim Period*, a troubled and obscure time which saw Egypt enter a long period of anarchy and social upheaval from about 2180 B.C. in the VIIth dynasty to about 2130 B.C. at the beginning of the XIth.

THE MIDDLE KINGDOM

The Middle Kingdom started about 2060 B.C. with the end of the XIth dynasty. The Pharaoh Montu-Hotep I re-established control over Lower Egypt with the aid of the Egyptian "middle class". During the reigns of his successors, Montu-Hotep II and Montu-Hotep III, commerce was intesified, a trade route to the Red Sea was opened and an expansionist policy aimed at Nubia was put into operation.

The XIIth dynasty had its beginnings about the year 2000 B.C. and it proved to be one of the most renowned and also one of the greatest in the whole of Egyptian history. Its first pharaoh was Amon-Emhat I who established the cult of Amon who consequently became the principal deity. This pharaoh was an able

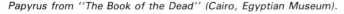

Papyrus from ''The Book of the Dead'' (Cairo, Egyptian Museum).

Ceremony of the weighing of the heart.

administrator and under his rule Egypt enjoyed another period of great prosperity. He extended Egypt's frontier into the heart of Nubia going as far as Korosko and he also fought the Libyans. He was succeeded by his son Sesostris I who seized the gold mines of Wadi Allaki. To ensure the continuity of the dynasty he associated his eldest son with the throne and all his successors followed his example. We have very few documents relating to the reigns of his successors Amon-Emhat II and Sesotris II but we do know established with Phenicia. The region around Feyyrum was reclaimed and Amon-Emhat III built a grandiose residence there which was so complex that the Greeks referred to it as the « Labyrinth ». His successor, Sesotris III, was one of Egypt's most important sovereigns. Following four military campaigns he colonised Nubia, he went as far as Palestine and he built a large number of forts along the frontier with the Sudan. During this period there was also a considerable flowering of cultural activity demonstrated by such famous works as the « Book of Two Lives » and the « Teachings of Amon-Emhat ».

With the XIIth dynasty the Middle Kingdom came to an end. It was succeeded by the so-called *Second Interim Period* which even today remains obscure and full of uncertainties. It was dominated by the invasion of a Semitic people coming from east of the Delta. The priest Manetonius of Sebennite who wrote a history of Egypt in Greek entitled « Memorable Facts about Egypt » called them Hyksos, a deformation of the Egyptian word « Hekakhasut » meaning « head of foreign countries ». They invaded the fertile plains of the Delta, fortified the city of Avaris and made it their capital. The victory of the Hiksos over the Egyptians must have been quite easy because not only did they find a weak government but they were also militarily superior to the Egyptians. They were responsible for the introduction of iron weapons, horses and war chariots all of which were previously unknown to the Egyptians, the Hyksos princes united around them other dynasties of Upper Egypt and defeated the invading army. This reconquest was brought to a successful conclusion around 1622 B.C. by Ahmose, also the founder of the XVIIIth dynasty, who chased the enemy as far as southern Palestine and reunited Egypt under his rule.

The colossus of Akhen Aton (Cairo, Egyptian Museum).

THE NEW KINGDOM

The New Kingdom which dates from about 1580 B.C. signaled the triumph of Egyptians arms over the whole of the then known world. It was a period of military power based not on defence but on conquest. It was also a period of great artistic achievement and of cultural activity in general. Thebes was still the capital and the priests of Amon were more influential than ever. Ahmose's immediate successors, Tutmose I and Tutmose II, devoted their reigns mainly to military expeditions and conquest. Queen Hatshepsut on the other hand was less war-like. She declared herself regent after removing her nephew Tutmose III and reigned alone for twenty two years, wearing a beard and male attire. Her reign, very quiet as far military activity was concerned, was characterised by frantic activity in the artistic sphere and in particular by the construction of the architectural master-piece constituted by the funerary complex at Deir-el-Bahari. At the death of this aunt Tutmose III regained the throne and had the name of the usurper erased from all her monuments. His 34 year reign turned out to be ont of the most splendid periods of Egyptian history. By means of seventeen military compaigns in Asia he defeated the Mitans conclusively. His victories at Megiddo, Karkhemish and Kadesh are famous. Toward the end of his reign Tutmose III reached the fourth cataract so that Egypt stretched from Napata in Nubia, now Gebel Barkal, to the river Euphrates. In 1372 B.C. Amon-Ofis IV ascended the throne. He has gone down in history as the poet-king and also as the heretical or schismatic king. Frightened by the power of the priests of Amon who had succeeded in creating a state within a state he substituted the worship of Aton, the solar disc, for that of Amon. This new cult did not require the use of images so he closed the temples and dispersed the clergy. He also abandoned Thebes and founded a new capital Akhet-Aton, « the horizon of Aton », now called Tell el-Amarna. His final act was to change his own name from Amon-Ofis, which means « Amon is pleased », to Akhen-Aton, which means « this pleases Aton ».

The religious change however did not survive him. The crown passed to the very young Tut-Ankh-Aton who under the influence of the beautiful Nefertiti, « the beautiful one who comes », wife-sister of Akhen-Aton, returned to Thebes after a short while, revived the cult of Amon and changed his own name to Tut-Ankh-Amon. This king who died mysteriously at the age of eighteen has passed into history because of the fascinating story of the discovery of his tomb in 1922 by Howard Carter. Egypt then fell into a state of anarchy and thence into the hands of military rulers: Horemheb, Ramses I, a professional soldier, Seti I who revived the policy of conquest to the east, and finally Ramses II, known as Ramses the Great, who engaged all his forces in order to defeat the armies of the Hittites. They were in fact stopped at Kadesh after an epic battle of doubtful outcome which had no real victors or vanquished. During his seventy seven year reign he enjoyed demonstrating his great power by building colossal monuments e.g. Abu Simbel, Karnak and Luxor. On his death he was succeeded by his son Mineptah. Internal anarchy together with the arrival towards the end of the second millenium B.C. of Indo-European peoples in Libya, Asia and the whole of the Mediterranean basin destroyed an already precarious equilibrium. The *Third Interim Period* started in 1085 B.C. with the advent of the XXIst dynasty when the capital, was at Tanis. The succeeding dynasty saw power first in the hands of a Libyan King and later in the hands of an Ethiopian king, the capital being moved to Nepatat in the Sudan. This was followed by the Saitian-Persian period. In 524 B.C. during the XVIIth dynasty the Persians under Cambyses conquered Egypt for the first time. In 332 B.C. the Egyptians called on Alexander the Great to help them and he was acclaimed as a Liberator. Declared « a son of Ra » by the oracle of Luxor he funded the new city of Alexandria (he was buried there in 323 B.C.) which rapidly became the cultural capital of the whole of the ancient world. His death marked the beginning of the Ptolemaic or lagidan dynasty which started the Hellenisation of the country. During the two centuries preceding the birth of Christ, Egypt became progressively weaker compared with Rome of which it eventually became a colony. Finally at the death of Theodosius in 595 A.D. Egypt became a part of the Eastern Empire.

Detail of a painting representing scenes from family life. (Valley of the Workmen - Tomb of Inherka).

THE SOCIETY OF ANCIENT EGYPT

The Pharaoh

Egypt was always an absolute monarchy, the king or Pharaoh was belived to be a god living on earth who, after his apparent death, would return to join the other deities. He bore the title « Child of the Sun » and represented religious, political and military power throughout Egypt. He was assisted by a « vizir » who was the head of the executive. The word « pharaoh » is in fact a Greek distortion of an Egyptian word referring to the royal palace. It was only in the New Kingdom from about 1580 B.C. that « pharaoh » came to mean the person of the sovereign himself.

Social and Administrative Constitution

The inhabitants of Egypt were divided into classes, the most respected being that of the priests charged with the upkeep of the temples. Rich and very influential, they were exempted from taxes and were maintained at the expense of the temple. The other classes were the nobility, charged with the higher levels of religious and political government of the provinces, the scribes or civil servants of the royal administration, and the people itself who were mainly peasants and artisans.

Agriculture

From the most remote periods Egypt has been an essentially agricultural country and it has always produced fruit, broad beans, lentils, flax and above all cereals, especially wheat and millet, which were exported in large quantities. As can be seen from the paintings of various periods which show work in the fields, the implements used have always been more or less the same as those used today.

Industry and Commerce

The Egyptians also practised the industrial arts and commerce. The large variety of objects found in the tombs shows that they were able to work gold, silver

Representation of a sun barge. (Valley of the Workmen).

and copper with rare skill and that in the cutting of precious stones they reached an incredible degree of perfection. They excelled particularly in the art of adornment (rings, bracelets, pendants, earrings) which reached a series of high points under the IVth, XIIth, XVIIIth and XXth dynasties. They produced textiles of great distinction from essentially very simple materials. They also made pottery, glass, and enamel. They did not use money. With the peoples of Nubia they exchanged the products of agriculture and industry, wheat and onions, arms and jewels, for woods and skins, gold and ivory. Spices and incense came from Arabia while from Phoenicia they imported cargoes of cedar wood.

From the XVIIIth dynasty on the Egyptians established close trading relations with the countries touched by the Euphrates and with the islands of the eastern Mediterranean. For example Cyprus furnished them with copper.

The Sciences

According to the teachings of the priest man acquired his ideas on science from Thot, the lunar god also called Hermes Trismegistus, a Greek name meaning « three times very great ». The social institutions of Ancient Egypt were attributed to another Hermes. Considered to be the inventor of writing he (Thot or Hermes the second?) wrote all his works under the inspiration of the Supreme God.

Ancient Egypt was very advanced in astronomy. From earliest times the Egyptians, following their observations of the motion of the celestial bodies, had used an astronomical year divided into three agricultural seasons of four months each corresponding to flooding, sowing and harvesting. To the total of 360 days thus obtained were added five extra days called « epagomeni » which were treated as major feast days. On the other hand as far as medicine was concerned we find that from earliest times it was associated with magic. Various medical texts, some on gynecology, some containing formulae and remedies, some on surgery, have come down to us.

Egyptian doctors were certainly familiar with the therapeutic value of some plants. On the other hand they did not have a very thorough knowledge of anatomy which is somewhat surprising in view of the fact that they practised mummification.

This is because of their religious beliefs which considered the body to be sacred.

EGYPTIAN RELIGION

The almost infinite varieties of representation of the numerous divinities which have been found in ancient Egyptian monuments have led to a gross misunderstanding about the religion of the Ancient Egyptians. The religion of ancient Egypt which one is tempted to think of as polytheistic, was in fact, like all the great religions, monotheistic. Today scholars are agreed that the many divinities found in Egyptian temples are to be considered as attributes or intermediaries of the Supreme Being, the One God, the only one recognized and worshipped by the priests, those initiates or wise men of the sanctuaries. At the pinnacle of the Egyptian pantheon there stands a God who is unique, immortal, who was not created, who is invisible and hidden in the inaccessible depths of his own Being. Begot by himself from all eternity he absorbs in himself all divine characheristics. It was not gods that were worshipped in Egypt but, under the name of whatsoever deity, the hidden God who has no name or form. A single idea dominated everything, that of a God who is one and primordial.

The Egyptian priests defined him thus: « He who is begotten from himself; the Principle of all life, the Father of fathers, the Mother of mothers » and they also said « From him comes the substance of all other gods » and « It is by His will that the sun shines, that the earth is separated from the firmament, and that harmony reigns on all creation ». However to make the belief in the One God more understandable to the Egyptian people, the priests expressed his attributes and his various roles by means of subtle representations. The most perfect image of God was the sun with its three attributes: shape, light and heat. The sun's soul was called Amon or Amon-Ra, a name which means « hidden-sun ». He is the father of life and the other divinities are only the different parts of his body. We can now introduce the famous Egyptian triads. Ad the masters of this ancient theogony tell us the

The god Khnum presents the kneeling Pharaoh to the god Amon (Abydos - Temple of Seti I).

Supreme Being, the creator of the universe, is unique in his being but not in his person. He does not come out of himself to beget but the begets within himself. He is at one and the same time the Father, the Mother and the Son of God without leaving God. These three persons are « God in God » and far from destroying the unity of the divine nature together they engender his infinite perfection. The Father represents creative power while the Son, image of the Father, strengthens and manifests his eternal attributes.

Every Egyptian province had its own triad, all interrelated, but this more compromised the divine unity than the division of Egypt into provinces compromised the unity of the central government. The principal or great triad was that of Abydos which consisted of Osiris, Isis and Horus. It was the most popular and was worshipped throughout Egypt because Osiris personified Good and was popularly known as the « good God ». The triad at Memphis consisted of Ptah, Sakhmet and Nefer-Tum, that at Thebes of Amon, Mut and Khonsu. The Trinity was not the only dogma which Egypt had retained from primitive revelation. In the holy books one also finds original sin, the promise of a redeeming God, future restorations of humanity, and the resurrection of the flesh at the end of time. At each change of dynasty there was a monotheistic revolution and the Supreme Being prevailed over the fetishism of the other divinities. The religious revolution of Akhnaton had been preceded by that of Menes, not to mention that of Osiris (5th millenium B.C.). According to some historians during the reign of Osiris, king of Thebes, (4200 B.C.) a complete change in religion occurred.

This king, the most devout of all, succeeded in getting monotheism adopted on a wide scale. It was this same Osiris, defied, who reigned over the supreme court for the judgement of the souls of the dead.

According to the rite of « psychostatis » (meaning « weighing of the soul », i.e. the ceremony of final judgement of the deceased), the soul of the dead person was carried on a sacred barge over the waters of the Elysian Fields. As the barge passed it brought light to those regions inhabited by the souls of the damned who trembled with joy at the sight of a little of that light which was now denied to them. The barge continued its journey and after crossing a lighter zone, corresponding more or less to our purgatory, finally reached the supreme court presided over by Osiris and his fourty two assessors. The heart of the dead person was placed in one pan of a balance while in the other was placed a feather, symbol of the goddness Maat. If the dead person had done more good than evil then they became one of the « true of voice » and thus a part of the mystical body of the god Osiris. If this was not so the heart was eaten by an animal with the head of a crocodile and the body of a hippopotamus and ceased to exist in the Other World. A soul which had thus been « justified » was then admitted to Ialou, the Elysian Fields.

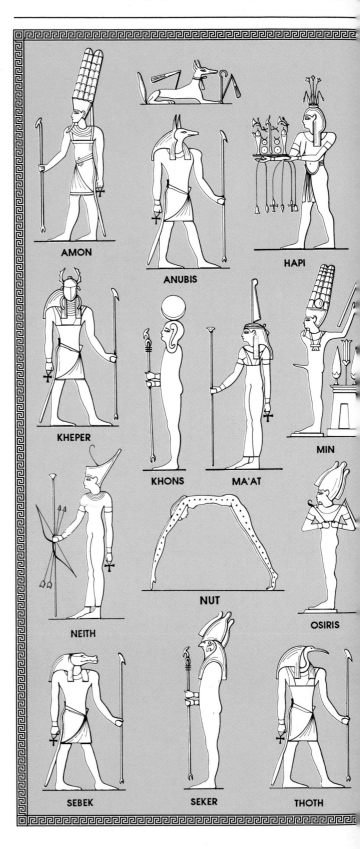

AMON

ANUBIS

HAPI

KHEPER

KHONS

MA'AT

MIN

NEITH

NUT

OSIRIS

SEBEK

SEKER

THOTH

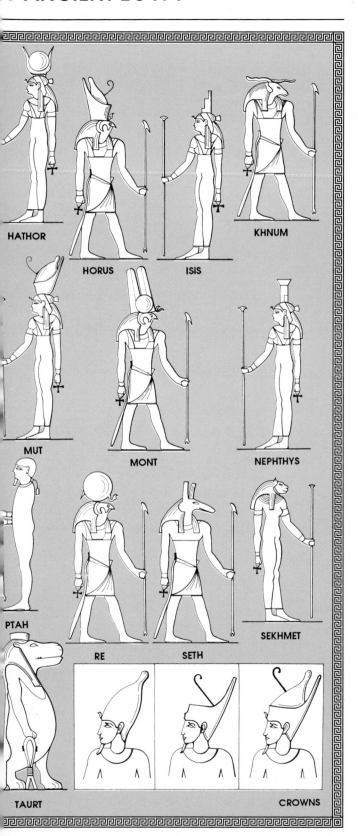

HATHOR
HORUS
ISIS
KHNUM
MUT
MONT
NEPHTHYS
PTAH
RE
SETH
SEKHMET
TAURT
CROWNS

At this point one may well ask why so many everyday objects are found in the pyramids and tombs. It should not be forgotten that the fundamental religious idea of the Ancient Egyptians was that human life continued even after physical death. But only those who continued to enjoy what they had enjoyed in the life could attain the Other World. Hence the house furnishings, the food, the drink, the servants and the other objects necessary to everyday life.

SACRED ANIMALS

To our eyes the monotheism of the all Ancient Egyptian religion has all the appearances of fetishism. However it should be recognized that the innumerable gods of the Egyptian pantheon are nothing more than manifestations of the Supreme Being in his different roles, agents or representations of the eternal aspect of the divinity. This is the meaning which must be attached to the cult of the sun, of the earth, even of certain animals, which one finds in different provinces of Egypt. Indeed it was only at a relatively late period that the Egyptian gods assumed a human appearance, initially they incarnated plants and animals. The goddes Hathor lived in a sycamore tree, the goddess Neith who gave birth while remaining a virgin and whom the Greeks identified with Athena was worshipped in the shape of a shield with two crossed arrows. Nefertum (identified in Prometheus) went under the form of a lotus flower.

But the Egyptian god appeared to the faithful predominantly in the form of an animal. A few examples will suffice: Horus is a sparrow-hawk, Thot an ibis, Bastet a cat, Khunm a ram. However apart from the gods who were personified by animals, there are the animals themselves who, when they had the right characteristics and bore certain special signs, were themselves worshipped. One of the most important examples of this behaviour was the elaborate cult of Apis, the sacred bull, at Memphis. In order to be recognized as sacred this animal had to possess certain characteristics known only to the priests. Following the death of an Apis the priests, after a long fast, set about finding a new Apis who had to have a white triangular mark on his forehead, a mark in the shape of an eagle on the neck and another mark like a crescent moon on its flank. At Memphis the animal lived in a stable in front of the world. There the animal received offerings from its worshippers and pronunced its oracles. Up until the XIXth dynasty each bull had its own burial place. However Ramses II created a common burial place for them, a special mausoleum called the Serapeum. This latter name arose because Apis once dead and deified became Osor-Apis which the Greeks made into Serphis. On the basis of certain precise indications contained in a passage of Strabonius, the French archeologist Auguste Mariette managed to find the mythical Serapeum at Sakkarah in 1851. It is a vast

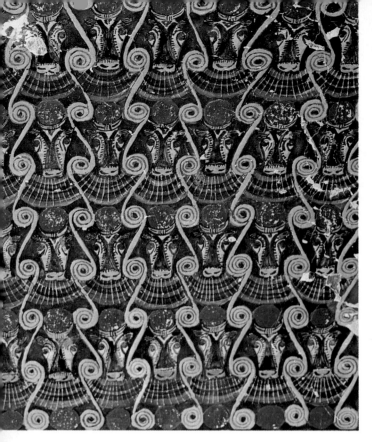

Detail of ceiling decorated with spiral forms and with the figure of the sacred ox Apis (Valley of the Workmen - Tomb of Inherka)

The goddess Hathor represented as a sacred cow. (Valley of the Queens - Tomb of Thiti).

underground construction, essentially a long corridor off which ran the burial chambers which contained monolithic sarcophagi of red granite, limestone or basalt which measured up to seventy tonnes and contained the mummies of the sacred bulls.

It was in recognition of the value of certain birds to agriculture that the Ancient Egyptians counted them among the sacred animals. At Sakkarah there is a necropolis for the ibis, the sacred bird par excellence, today a disappearing species. The denuded head and neck of the ibis should be blue-black feathers on the wings. Whilst alive it was dedicated to the god Thot whom the Greeks called Hermes, whilst once dead it was mummified and placed in a clay vase.

At Thebes there was a very special cult of the crocodile which lived there quite tame with ear-rings in its ears and gold rings on its toes. This was not so in all towns and Herodotus reports that the inhabitants of Elephantine and its surroundings did not at all consider the crocodile sacred and had no scruples about eating it!

The cat also played a big role in Egyptian religion.

The female cat was dedicated to the goddess Bast and personified the beneficial heat of the sun. Its cult was practised particularly in Lower Egypt and the city of Bubaste, today Zigazag, owed its name to a temple dedicated to this goddess. The cat was considered so sacred than anyone killing one, even accidentally, was

put to death. A great number of embalmed cats were found at Beni Hassan.

THE IMMORTALITY OF THE SOUL

All the books on the After-life demonstrate that the immortality of the soul was fundamental to the ancient Egyptians'religious beliefs. Pyramids, mastabas and tombs were all constructed to house the souls of the dead. The word « Ka » indicates the universal spirit, the physical body which animates the entire being.

After the death of the body, the soul enfolds the mummy; it becomes its « Ka », its « double » until the spirit is trasformed into « astral spirit » and « Ka » and « Ba » (the divine spark, one of the spiritual principles of the individual) become one, uniting through Osiris' cord with the superior spirit to form one single spirit. Numerous frescoes representing the immortality of the soul and other religious scenes have been found in the brick dwellings which housed the Pharaohs. In all the funerary temples and in the tombs were depicted scenes symbolising the survival of the deceased in the afterworld, in eternal life; for this they were called « houses of eternity ». « Ankh », the crux ansata, also symbolised the life to come with its three attributes: peace, happiness and serenity.

FUNERAL PRACTICES AND MUMMIFICATION

The art of embalming bodies and trasforming them into mummies was believed to be of divine origin and to go back to Horus the son of Osiris and Isis.

The term mummy comes from the Arabic « mumiya » or « mumyai » which according to the 12th century Arab traveller Adb-el-Latif refers to bitumen or a mixture of pitch and myrrh, a material which was extensively used in the treatment of corpses and which was an important item of commerce even in medieval Europe. At one time a careful distinction was made between natural and artificial mummies, the former category being those which remained intact without treatment. Even today it is believed that the spectacular state of conservation of Egyptian mummies is due more to the extremely arid Egyptian climate, with the resulting total absence of bacteria in the air and sand, than to the enbalming process.

Thanks to the presence of well preserved bas-reliefs and paintings in the tombs we have a very good idea of how funerals were conducted in ancient Egypt. Opening the funeral procession would be a group of slaves carrying offerings and objects belonging to the dead man. If he had been a warrior there would be his neapons, if he had been a farmer there would be his farming implements. Next would come a group of professional mourners uttering piercing cries, tearing their hair and singing dirges. Finally behind the master of ceremonies and the priest would be the catafalque in the shape of a solar barge, mounted on a sledge drawn by a team of oxen. Family, friends and relatives followed, dressed in mourning, uttering cries and lamentations. Right at the back of the procession would be a group of women singing the praises of the dead man. Along the way would be gathered the idle

Representation of the god Anubis leaning over a mummy.
(Valley of the Workmen - Tomb of Sennedjen).

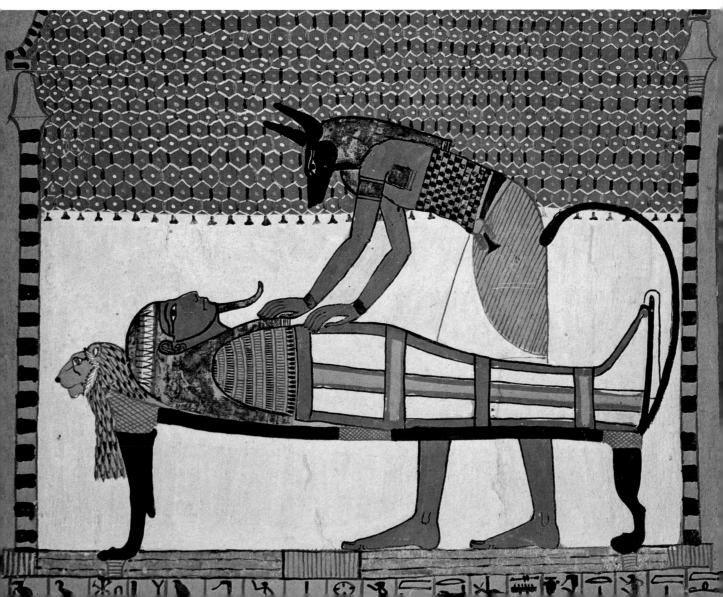

and the curious. If the cemetery was on the other bank of the Nile, the funeral procession would cross the river, the catafalgue would be placed once again on its sledge and the different groups would form up again in the same order. When finally they arrived at the tomb the mummy would receive the offerings and the final good-byes of family and friends. There then followed the « ceremony of the opening of the eyes and mouth » by means of which the dead person had their senses restored to them. The mummy would then be laid in the tomb.

We shall now look into the question of how the body was mummified. The body of the dead man was handed over to specialists who proceeded to embalm it. The first operation consisted of extracting the brain via the nostrils by means of a hooked tool. The brain cavity was then filled with a material consisting mainly of liquid bitumen which hardened on cooling. The eyes were then removed and replaced by porcelain substitutes. By means of a sharp stone an incision was then made in the left side of the body and the intestines and internal organs removed. These were treated with boiling bitumen and wrapped up. The brain and the liver were treated in a similar way. The viscera were preserved in four canopic jars made of clay, limestone or alabaster, in some cases even of stone or metal depending on the station of the dead man. These jars which were placed in a coffer near the mummy had lids each of which had a different head on it: man, jackal, sparrow-hawk and dogfaced baboon. The cavities in the gut and stomach were carefully washed with palm wine, dried with a powdered mixture of aromatic plants and finally filled with myrrh or perfumed sawdust. The body thus prepared was placed in a solution of natron (sodium carbonate) and left for seventy days. After this treatment the flesh and muscles had completely dissolved away and nothing remained except the skin attached to the bones. The hair of men was cut short while that of women was left in all its splendour.

Bandages impregnated with resin were wound round each finger then round the hand and finally round the arm. The same procedure was carried out on the other limbs. For the head even greater care was taken. The cloth in direct contact with the skin was rather like muslin. The face was covered with several layers of this material and the degree of adhesion was so perfect that when removed as a whole it could be used as a mold to make a plaster cast of the dead man's features. The whole body was then wrapped up in the same way. The body was arranged in an extended position either with the hands crossed on the breast or with the arms extended along the flanks. The bodies of the pharaohs were wrapped in a sheath of repoussé gold work which reproduced the shape of the body in relief. The state of preservation of the mummies in the Egyptian museums in Cairo and Alexandria as well as those in foreign museums is pretty well perfect. The oldest known mummy is that of Sekkeram-Saef, son of Pepi I (IVth dynasty) which was discovered at Sakkarah, near Memphis, in 1881 and which is now in the Cairo Museum. The great skill of the embalmers has thus enabled the likenesses of the great pharaohs to be transmitted to us down the centuries.

In the withered head of Mernefta, believed by many to be the pharaoh of the Jewish Exodus, we can still recognize the characteristic family nose as well as the eyebrows which are still quite thick.

In that of Ramses II X-ray examination has shown that he undoubtedly had trouble with his teeth.

Detail of voyage of the deceased to Abydos.
(Valley of the Nobles - Tomb of Kiki).

An example of papyrus kept in
the British Museum in London.

HIEROGLYPHIC WRITING

Right from the beginning the deciphering of the mysterious Egyptian writing fascinated everybody. In 1799 a certain Captain Bouchard of the Franch Army was supervising work on the fortifications of Fort St. Julian, situated a little more than four kilometres outside the town of Rosetta when his workmen discovered a stone which was destined to achieve great fame in archeological history. It was in fact the « Rosetta Stone » which led to the deciphering of the hieroglyphs.

As a result of the fortunes of war this precious stone fell into the hands of the British who gave it a place of honour in the British Museum. On one face of the stone, a tablet of extremely hard black basalt, there is a long trilingual inscription, the three texts being written one above the other. The first of the inscriptions, 14 lines long, is written in hieroglyphs. The second, 32 lines long, is written in demotic, from the Greek word « demos » meaning people, which refers to a type of script used by ordinary people. (Demotic is contrasted wth hieratic, from « hieros » meaning sacred, whose use was restricted to priests and scholars). The third inscription, 54 lines long, is in Greek and hence was comprehensible. This latter text, translated without difficulty, proved to be a priestly decree in honour of

Ptolemy Epiphanes which finishes with a formal instruction that « this decree, engraved on a tablet of hard stone, in three srcripts, hieroglyphic, demotic and Greek, shall be engraved in each of the great temples of Egypt ».

The honour of deciphering the hieroglyphs fell to two scholars, the Englishman Thomas Young and the Frenchman François Champollion who started work on it at almost the same time and who were to see their efforts crowned with success. However Champollion probably has a greater right than his rival to be regarded as the man who deciphered the hieroglyphs. What Young achieved by instinct Champollion achived by scientific method and with such success that by his death in 1832 he could leave behind him a grammar and a very substantial dictionary of ancient Egyptian. But what did this writing that the Greeks called hieroglyphic, from « hiero glyphica », that is « sacred signs », actually consist of? The ancient Egyptians themselves called their written texts « the words of the gods ». In fact according to tradition men were taught to write by the god Thot himself during the reign of Osiris. Down through the centuries the writing retained a sacred character and more or less magical powers. Anybody who knew how to write the approxi-

15

mately seven hundred signs which constituted Egyptian writing, each sign representing a sound or an object, was held in great esteem. The names of the kings and queens were surrounded by an outline which archeologists call a « cartouches ». It was precisely from the names of Cleopatra and Ptolemy, engraved inside their « cartouches » on the Rosetta Stone, that Champollion started his long work on the deciphering of the hieroglyphs. The ancient Egyptians either engraved the hieroglyphs in the stonework of their temples or painted them on the walls of the burial chambers or inscribed them with a reed pen on rolls of papyrus, the antecedent of our paper.

What is papyrus? Papyrus is a perennial grass, a species of reed whose stem can range in height from two to five metres and which is terminated by an umbrellashaped flower. The white spongy pith of the stem was cut into thin sections which were laid out on a flat surface and stuck together at the edges. Then a second layer was laid on top of the first in a direction at right angles to it, the whole was then wetted and allowed to dry in the sun. This constituted leaf which was pressed and then scraped to make it thinner. Several sheets would be joined together to produce a long strip which could then be rolled up. The writing on the roll was presented in columns.

THE NILE

The Nile winds its way 6,500 kilometres from its origins in the Great African lakes to the Mediterranean. Its sources were unknown until the 19th century. Today thay have been identified in the Nyawarongo river, a tributary of another river which enters Lake Victoria.

The Nile flows northwards across the immense savannah with its woods and marshes before gathering in to itself from the left the waters of the Bahr Ghazzal (the Gazelle River) originating in the Darfour and Congo regions, and from the right the waters of the Sobat, the Blue Nile (or Bahr el Azrak) and the Atbarah from the high plateaus of Abyssinia. It then runs up against the limestone barrier of the Sahara and its progress is interrupted by the cataracts as it flows slowly towards the Mediterranean without receiving the waters of any other tributary. Egypt proper is simply that northern part of this great valley which extends from the

A felucca glides silently along the Nile at Aswan; the Aga Kahn's mausoleum is in the background. ►

Life in the fields. ►

The famous « Rosetta Stone » kept in the British Museum in London.

Detail of columns of hieroglyphic symbols (Valley of the Queens - Tomb of Amon-her-Khopechef).

cataracts at Aswan to the sea. From Aswan to the ruins of Thebes the valley narrows, being penned in between two chains of rocky mountains, but between Thebes and Cairo it becomes considerably wider again.

At El Manach the Nile divides into two: the eastern part constitues the principal branch. Shortly after the Nile leaves Cairo it loses sight of the mountains which up to then have followed its course. The Arabian and Libyan mountains get further and further apart and rise up respectively on the edge of the Red Sea and in the Mediterranean to the west of Alexandria. In the vast triangular plain of the Delta a multitude of canals link the Rachid or Rosetta branch to the Damiette or Domiatte branch.

Each year following the torrential rains which fall on the mountains of Abyssinia and the region of the equatorial lakes, the Nile becomes more and more swollen until finally it bursts its banks and in a few months fills up the entire valley. By the end of April the flooding has reached Khartoum, the capital of the Sudan, and by the end of May or beginning of June it reaches Egypt proper via Nubia. Until October the valley remains covered with the beneficial layer of mud laid down by the flood which only disappears completely at the beginning of December. As a result of this periodic flooding Egypt has a particularly rich flora and fauna. There are many types of big trees, numerous species of acacia and sycamore, forests of palm trees and many aquatic plants including the papyrus and the lotus. The Nile and its lakes are swarming with fish. Most domestic animals have been known in Egypt since the earliest times. On the other hand many species of wild animal have disappeared with the passing of the centuries. Thus one no longer finds there either lions or the large cats such as the leopard and the cheetah. The hippopotamus left the Delta towards the end of the 16th century and following the appearance of steam boats on the river it retreated beyond the cataracts as did the crocodile. If it were not for the flooding of the Nile the great Egyptian valley would be a sterile desert. This is why Herodotus's statement that « Egypt is a gift of the Nile » continues to be as true today as when he said it.

PRIMITIVE IRRIGATION

The system of irrigation in Egypt is primitive and most of the work has to be done manually. The major problem is that of raising the water from the river to the level of the banks. The land slopes away from the river, doubtless as a result of the annual alluvion, so that there is nothing easier, once the water has been raised to the level of the bank, than to send it down the channels right to the edge of the river in the period when its waters have withdrawn to its natural bed. The water

The ancient system of irrigation is still in use in Egypt.

A view of the Nile at Cairo.

is generally 4 or 5 metres below the level of the land and soon it will be even lower. To overcome this difference in levels use is made of the creaking « sakhyeh », a water wheel usually operated by asses or oxen. Alternatively water can be drawn from the Nile by means of the « shadoof », a simple leather bucket which is dipped in the river, filled with water and then raised by means of a counterweight, consisting of other buckets, at various levels, unitl the water finally reaches the field.

It has been calculated that this device can lift about 50 litres of water a minute, and pictures in Egyptian tombs prove that it has been in use on the banks of the Nile for more than three thousand years. No one has ever thought of improving it in spite of all the innovations and conquests of technology.

THE EGYPTIAN CLIMATE

Egypt could be described as a large oasis between two deserts. Although nature has divided it into two parts only, it theoretically can be divided into three parts: Upper, Middle and Lower Egypt. On the other hand there are only two seasons: the hot season which runs from April to October and the cool season which runs from November to the end of March. The felleh or peasant recognizes three distinct periods in the course of the year: Chetoui (winter), Sefi (summer) and Nili (the period of maximum flooding).

It is essentially a Saharan climate with almost no atmospheric precipitation and big changes in temperature between night and day. The temperature begins to rise at the beginning of March and this is when the « khamsin », a warm wind from the desert, also called « cherd » by the native Egyptians, « merissi » by the Bedouin and « simoun » by the inhabitants of the desert. The « khamsin » blows from the south west and its presence is announced by a sharp fall in the atmospheric pressure accompanied by a sudden rise in temperature. In a few minutes the thermometer can rise by 12 to 15° C., while the wind is accompanied by a fine cloud of dust whipped up from the desert. In Upper Egypt, especially at Luxor and Philae, the thermometer sometimes rises to 46° or even 48°C.

◄ *The Cairo Tower at Gezirah.*

A part of the Nile at Cairo.

CAIRO

Egypt was the first state to establish a system of administration and a capital with the administrative and religious centres.

During the late Predynastic Period, Confederations started to emerge with political heads or kings and a capital. In Lower or Northern Egypt, the capital was Buto in the heart of the Delta. The king wore a red crown with a cobra ad an emblem. In Upper or Southern Egypt, the capital was Nekheb between Aswan and Luxor; the king of which wore a white crown with a vulture as an emblem. The papyrus plant and its flower were the symbol of the North, while the lotus plant and its flower were the symbol of the South.

Then came the unity between the North and the South under the reign of King Menes (or Narmer) who chose Memphis between the north and the south to be the first capital of unified Egypt. Memphis is 22 km from Cairo.

The best place for the foundation of the Egyptian capital was always the point before the Nile branches. The capital of Egypt has changed throughout history from Ahnasia south of Memphis to Thebes (Luxor).

When Alexander the Great entered Egypt in 332 B.C., the capital was transferred west of the Delta to Alexandria. Christianity was introduced and the seat of the Patriarch was between Alexandria and old Cairo.

Alexandria remained the Egyptian capital during both the Ptolemaic and Roman periods.

In 639 A.D. Amr Ibn El As entered Egypt and introduced Islam. He wanted to keep Alexandria as the capital of egypt but Khalif Omar Ibn Al Khatab ordered him to build a new city. He founded Al Fustat in 641 A.D. beside the fortress of Babylon as the first Islamic capital of Egypt.

When the Abbassides took over from the Ommayades in 750, Saleh Ibn Ali abandoned Al Fustat and established Al Askar north of the former capital. This new military capital developed and constituted with Al Fustat a big city.

Ahmed Ibn Touloun founded the third Islamic capital Al Qatai around his gigantic mosque in 870. This city had also a military character, with its high walls and circular road, with Al Askar and Al Fustat, it rapidly grew into one city.

When Gohar Al Sikkily, the Fatimid commander entered Egypt, he built the new city of Al Qahira or Cairo in 969 and from then on it became the capital of Egypt and the heart of Islam.

Since the foundation of Al Fustat and until the construction of Cairo, capital cities were always constructed to the north. There-

21

Mohammed Ali Mosque: a side of the courtyard and the fountain for ablutions.

fore Al Qahira was constructed north of the three cities built by the Arabs. This is the beginning of a long period during which the city grew in size. In effect a new capital developed quickly and passed its limits.

The arrival of Salah El Din in 1176 marked a different stage in the history of Cairo. During the Ayyùbid era, the Citadel was built and work began on building a wall surrounding the cities forming Al Qahira. The Mamlùkes era (1250-1517) was a period of great construction and town planning in Cairo. The Ottomans (1517-1798) continued the development. The Mamlùkes began adding big commercial activities. During the reign of Mohamed Ali and his successors, the city developed considerably.

After the revolution of 1952, and in the sixties, there was great demographic growth in Cairo.

Greater Cairo today is home to twelve million inhabitants, and is composed of three governorates: Cairo, Giza and Qalyobia, as well

as twenty eight quarters.

The average population density is 50.000 inhabitants/km².

The historical capital is considered the most populated African city. It is also a great political, cultural and economic centre in the Middle East.

MOHAMED ALI MOSQUE

Mohamed Ali Mosque is the emblem of the Cairo Governorate. Mohamed Ali (1769-1849) was born in Cavalia, Greece, and was of Albanian origin. He was a soldier in the troops that were sent to Egypt to free the country from Napoleon's occupation and took part in the land battle of Abou Kir on the 25th of July 1799. In 1808 he was the commander of the Albanian troops in Egypt.

In 1805 the Egyptians revolted against Wali Khourshid and Mohamed Ali took over.

The mosque was built in 1830 in two parts: the mosque and the courtyard.

The court measures 52×54 m and is surrounded by four corridors lined with marble columns and surmounted by little domes. In the centre of the court there is the fountain for ablutions (where Muslims wash before saying their prayers that take place five times a day). The clock tower on the western side of the fountain is of perforated copper. The clock was a present from King Louis-Philippe of France to Mohamed Ali Pasha in the year 1845.

Architect Youssef Boshna from Turkey who constructed this mosque, took his model from the Hagia Sophia, the church that was later transformed into a mosque, and is known for its Byzantine style.

The mosque is square in shape, the length of its side is 41 m, the central dome is 21 m in diameter and 52 m high. It is supported by 4 square pillars and surrounded by 4 semi-domes and the semidome of the kibla.

On the western side of the mosque stand two cylindrical minarets (pencil minarets) in the Ottoman style. The height of each is 84 m. This mosque is characterized by the great quantities of alabaster that adorn the walls. The pulpit (minbar) and the dekka (tribune) are made of white marble. The mihrab is covered with alabaster and gold decorations.

A large number of pendant glass and crystal lamps form circles of lighting inside the mosque.

Tomb of Mohamed Ali Pasha

The three tiered tomb of Mohamed Ali Pasha is at the right side of the entrance door of his mosque. It is made of white marble, decorated with carved floral motifs and covered with painted and gilded inscriptions.

MOSQUE OF SULTAN HASSAN

This is one of the most beautiful and monumental mosques in Cairo. The builder of this mosque and school was Sultan El Nasser Hassan. He was the 19th of the Turkish Sultans to have reigned in Egypt and the seventh son of the Sultan El Nasser Mohamed Ibn Kalaoun.

Conspiracies were one of his era's traits. He decided to build his mosque in the square facing the Citadel of Salah El Din. He began the construction in 1356 and it was completed in the year 1363 by Bashir Agha who was one of his princes. This mosque is considered one of the greatest works of Islamic architecture. The mosque is 7907 square meters wide. The entrance is 37.80 m high.

There is also a schoool or a madrassa mosque for the four rites of Islam.

The court is almost a square in shape. Each side is about 32 meters in length. On each side there is an wan that stands higher than the court. Each wan is roofed with a brick-pointed tunnel-vault with a stone arch. Art lovers consider the arches of its largest wan a miracle of construction.

The walls of the Iwan are covered with coloured stone blocks and marble. There is a stucco inscription containing verses from Surat El Fath in Kufic writing. In the middle of the wan there is a marble pulpit and tribune of great craftsmanship. Around the mihrab there are four marble supports.

On the right side of the minbar, which is made of white marble, there is a wooden door covered with bronze. At each side of the qibla wall there is a door. The two doors lead to the tomb chamber. The doors were covered with bronze and gold silver inlay.

The tomb chamber is 21 square

Left: the Mosque of Sultan Hassan; right: the Mosque of Al Rifai.

meters high. The walls are covered with marble up to 8 meters.

The Mosque of Sultan Hassan has two minarets. One is 82 meters high and is considered one of the highest Islamic minarets. It is two meters shorter than the two minarets of Mohamed Ali Pasha Mosque which was built 500 years later.

STATUE OF RAMSES II

The statue was found in Memphis, and then taken to Cairo in 1954, to be exhibited in the station square. It is 10 meters high and the double crown represents the unity between the North and the South. On the back of the statue there is a stanchion bearing the Pharaoh's titles, one of which is « The Strong Ox » which is the symbol of fertility. Between the statue's legs is a relief of Ramses' wife (Bent-Anath) daughters and one of his three daughters who were given this title. A replica of this statue stands now on the road leading to Cairo Airport.

THE EGYPTIAN MUSEUM

The French Egyptologist, Mariette Pasha, insisted on the construction of a big museum to house the Pharaonic works of art. Twenty years later, the French architect Marcel Dourgnon presented the plan of the Egyptian Museum building situated in the centre of Cairo. The museum was opened in 1902 and Gasto Maspero was appointed Director. The museum contains a big library and 100 exhibition rooms occupyng two floors. In the museum's garden, there is a big bronze statue over the marble tomb of Auguste Mariette bearing his name and dates of birth and death (1821-1881). There is also a number of statue's representing other famous Egyptologists. The most important collection of the museum is that of Tutankhamun. There are other masterpieces dating from the Ancient Kingdom like the Statues of Cheops, Chepren and Mycerinus. There is also the collection of Thutmose III, Alhnatoun and a number of statues of Ramses II.

The statue of Ramses II in the Station Square, Cairo.

The main entrance to the Egyptian Museum

Two statues on either side of the gate represent the symbols of the North and the South of Ancient Egypt. One is holding the lotus and the other the papyrus.

The gold coffin of Tutankhamon

The gold coffin of Tutankhamon is made of 450 pounds of solid gold. It is, perpaps, the finest and greatest example of goldsmithing work in history. Three coffins were used to hold the body of young king Tutankhamon who died at the age of 18. The inner and outer coffins are displayed among his collection in the Egyptian Museum in Cairo. King Tut's tomb was discovered on November 4, 1922 by Howard Carter, after six years of hard work underneath the rubble that heaped up during the excavation of King Ramses VI tomb, in Thebes, Valley of the Kings.

King Mentuhotep (Dynasty XI)

This is a rare statue of Pharaoh Mentuhotep of the 11th dynasty. It is one of a group of eight statues that were found in his mortuary temple at Deir Al Bahary, west of Luxor, beside Queen Hatshepsut's temple built five centuries later.

The sandstone statue, which is 2.3 meters high, represents the Pharaoh seated in the Osiris position wearing a white costume with his crown painted red. The colour of the body under the white cloak is olive black. The statue was found wrapped in bandages like a mummy and placed in a funerary niche in his monumental temple.

Dwarf Seneb and his family (Dynasty VI)

The ancient Egyptian sculptor excelled in this piece of work of the Dwarf Seneb, who was an important official, and his family. He portrayed Dwarf Seneb with his wife holding him with her right arm and their two children in the place of the dwarf's short legs. This group is made of painted limestone and was found in Seneb's tomb in Giza north of Chephren's pyramid.

Sheikh El Balad (Dynasty V)

This is the most famous wooden statue belonging to the Old Kingdom. It is the statue of the noble Kaaper who was also known as the great priest. You can see the dignity reflected on his features. The eyes are made of quartz embedded in copper lids. It is made of a single block of sycamore wood, apart from the arms. When it was found in 1860 near Sakkarah, it reminded the workers who discovered it of their « Chief of the Village » or à Sheikh El Balad », the mayor's assistant, hence its name.

The Scribe (Dynasty IV)

Ancient Egyptians considered the profession of the scribe to be the highest of professions. The scribe was close to the Pharaoh because of his wisdom and knowledge. This statue is made of painted limestone and is of an unknown squatting scribe holding an open papyrus roll on his knees. The eyes are of inlaid quartz and framed with bronze. Although the ancient Egyptian was very careful to keep up with artistic standards in sculpture, there is a little deviation of the statue's head to the right side as if thinking before writing.

Prince Rahotep and his wife Nofret (Dynasty IV)

This statuary group that was found in the tomb of Rahotep in Meidum represents Prince Rahotep, who was high priest of Heliopolis, and his wife Princess Nofret. They are carved out of two separate blocks of limestone, but were meant to be seen toghether. They are both painted, with inlaid eyes and in an excellent state of preservation. One can notice that usual distinction in colour between the skin of men and women thet was usually made by ancient Egyptians.

A group of black granite (Dynasty XVIII)

This is a group of black granite representing the mayor Senefer of Thebes sitting beside his wife Senetnay with their daughter Mutneferet between them. It dates back to the 18th dynasty during the reign of Amenhotep II.

GIZEH

Before describing the imposing and famous funerary complex at Gizeh we might look at what that famous Greek «journalist», Herodotus, had to say about it on the basis of the testimony of various foreigners who had lived in Egypt. Although Herodotus often criticized Egypt and its inhabitants he nevertheless left us an incredible amount of precious information.

He writes «Cheops left behind him a colossal piece of work, his pyramid. Up to the reign of Rhampsinitus, Egypt was excellently governed and very prosperous. Cheops, his successor, compelled his subjects to labour as slaves for him. Some were forced to drag blocks of stone from the quarries in the Arabian hills to the Nile, where they were ferried across and taken over by others who hauled them to the Libyan hills. The work went on in three-monthly shifts, a hundred thousand men in a shift.

It took ten years to build the track along which the blocks were hauled, a work of hardly less magnitude than the pyramid itself, for it is 5 stadia long (923.5 metres), 10 orgyia wide (18.47 metres) and 8 orgyia high (14.78 metres) at its highest point, and is constructed of polished stone blocks decorated with carvings of animals. It took ten years to build, including the underground burial chambers on the hill where the pyramids stand. A cut was made from the Nile, so that the water so deviated turned the site of the pyramid itself took twenty years. It is square at the base, the length of each side, 8 plethras (246.26 metres), being equal to the height. It is made of polished , beautifully fitted, stone blocks none of the blocks being less than 30 feet long (9.24 metres).»

General view of the three pyramids of Cheops, Chephren and Micerinus.

After this introduction Herodotus recounts the story of the building of the Great Pyramid, giving us the most precise details, from the typically Egyptian stylistic characteristics to the costs involved for the work on this strange edifice. «The pyramid was constructed in tiers or steps, something like battlements, and when the base was completed the remaining blocks were lifted by a kind of crane made of short timbers onto the first tier. On this first tier there was another lifting-crane which raised the blocks a stage higher, then yet another which raised them higher still. Each tier had its own crane or it may be that they used the same one which, being easy to carry, they shifted up from stage to stage as soon as its load was dropped into place. I describe the two procedures given in the two versions which I have heard about.

The finishing off of the pyramid started at the top and worked downwards, ending with the parts nearest the ground. An inscription on the pyramid in Egyptian characters records the amounts spent on horse-radish, onion and heads of garlic, and if I remember correctly what the interpreter who read me the inscription said, the sum involved was 1600 talents of silver (41,884 kilogrammes). If this is true how much must have been spent on the iron used, on other foodstuffs and on the clothing of the labourers? Not to mention the time it took, which cannot have been negligible, to quarry and haul the stone and to build the underground burial chamber».

Four centuries after Herodotus the historian Diodorus of Sicily (1st

The Kefren pyramid.

century B.C.) visited Egypt and in his turn visited the pyramids which he considered to be among the seven wonders of the world. Like his predecessor, Diodorus was filled with amazement in front of this monument. «One must agree» he wrote, «that these monuments are superior to everything else one sees in Egypt not only because of their enormous size and the prodigious sums which were spent on them but because of the beauty of their construction».

Diodorus then gives us his version of how the pyramids were built. His account speaks of all three great pyramids which he presents as being a funerary ensemble of the IVth dynasty. The Great Pyramid is only one element of this ensemble, albeit the most prestigious element, and it cannot be studied or understood out of this context. Like Herodotus, Diodorus of Sicily evaluates the sum spent on horse-radish, onions and garlic for the labourers on the Great Pyramid at 1600 talents, but unlike Herodotus he believed that these monuments did not contain the bodies of the pharaohs which, in his version, had been buried in safe and secret hiding places. We shall not cite further Diodorus's text which agrees, more or less, with that of Herodotus. We have only cited him at all in order to show that the greatest writers of antiquity were all equally impressed by the beauty and uniqueness of the Egyptian funerary monuments.

At Gizeh the visitor is presented with one of the most beautiful sights created by the hand of man. It is here that the Egyptian saying «Everybody fears Time but Time

The pyramid of Mykerinus and the three pyramids of the queens.

◄ *Two details of the pyramid of Cheops.*

fears the pyramids» is most apposite. Gizeh is the present name given to the great necropoli of Cairo and it consists of a plateau having an area of about two thousand square metres. The Sphinx together with the three Great Pyramids, those of Cheops, Chephren and Micerinus are found here. The latter has three small satellite pyramids. The three monuments are arranged diagonally but in such a way that none of them hides the sun from the other two. Typically each pyramid consists of a funerary temple in the valley. The complex of Cheops is almost completely destroyed while that of Chephren is largely extant. The pyramid of Cheops is the largest of the three. It was originally 146 metres high, today it is only 137 metres high, its truncated summit being a platform 10 metres square. Today the pyramid has completely lost its external facing, thus revealing the enormous internal blocks of stone over which one must laboriously climb in order to reach the summit. However the stupendous view from the top makes the effort involved well worth while. Chephren's pyramid is the only one

The solar bark.

THE SOLAR BARK

which still has, at least at the top the smooth external facing. Although it was lower than Cheop's today it is in fact the same height because it is not truncated. It originally had a red granite facing at the base.

Finally there is the smallest of the three, that of Micerinus, barely 66 metres high but of fairly regular dimensions. In the 16th century it still had its granite facing which today has completely disappeared. The burial chamber once contained a splendid sarcophagus of basalt, decorated in a manner common during the period of the Old Kingdom and called «palace faced». Unfortunately it was lost off the coast of Portugal when the ship carrying it to England was wrecked. In front of Micerinus's pyramid there are three satellite pyramids, even smaller than those of Cheops. The one to the east, originally covered in red granite, was probably intended for the wife of the pharaoh Kharmer-Nehty II. The poor state of preservation of Micerinus's funerary complex is due to the fact that some parts of it were finished in rather more haste than anticipated using unfinished brick and as a result it rapidly decayed.

In 1954 the Egyptian archaeologist Kamel el Mallak discovered two large pits south of the pyramid of Cheops. They were covered by enormous limestone blocks wich bore the cartouches of the pharaoh who succeeded Cheops, his son Dediefre. Upon removing one of the stones, a « solar bark » once more saw the light of day. It may even be the one which had accompanied the body of Cheops to Gizeh before he was buried in the great pyramid which the pharaoh had built as his eternal dwelling.

After over ten years of patient work, the boat, once more reconstructed in its original forms, was placed in the museum built expressly to house it next to the pyramid.

Two views of the Sphinx.

THE SPHINX

About 350 metres from Cheops's pyramid stands the Great Sphinx, known in Arabic as Abu el-Hol which means «father of terror». Seventy three metres long, this colossal statue represents a lion with a human head which some believe to be a likeness of Chephren standing guard over his tomb. Originally the Sphinx was called Hor-em-Akhet, which means «Horus who is on the horizon», from which the Greeks derived the name Harmakis. Many times during the course of the centuries the body of the Sphinx has

This is how David Roberts portrayed the Sphinx between 1846 and 1850.

A detail of the Sphinx's head, effigies of King Kefren.

been completely covered by the sand leaving only its enigmatic features (5 metres high) uncovered. Many times too men dug it out of the sand. The most renowned restoration was that of Tutmose IV who was ordered in a dream by Harmakis to uncover the Sphinx. The defacement of this mythical man-animal which is evident today is due in part to erosion by the wind and in part to the cannon of the Mamelukes who used it for target practice.

General view of the step-pyramid of Zoser.

SAKKARAH

The necropolis at Sakkarah which stretches for eight kilometres is the largest in the whole of Egypt. It is also historically the most important because the principal dynasties are all represented, from the Ist to the Ptolemaic and the Persian. The necropolis is under the special protection of the god Sokar, hence the name of the locality, who is often represented as green with a hawk-headed appearance.

In the middle of the necropolis is the funerary complex of Zoser, the pharaoh who founded the IIIrd dynasty, and around it can be found other pyramids and mastabas characteristic of the various

eras. The whole area is dominated by Zoser's huge step pyramid. To fully appreciate the importance and originality of this pyramid it is necessary to explain what is meant by a «mastaba» which in the Arabic language means a bench. A mastaba was the burial chamber of the nobility and of court dignitaries and it was rectangular with slightly inclined walls. Zoser was the first pharaoh to entrust an architect with the construction of a grandiose funerary complex. This architect, who was called Imhotep and whose name can be found inscribed in hieroglyphic characters on the base of a statue representing Zoser, was thus historically the first architect to receive official recognition and his ingenious structure was the first funerary

pyramid to appear in the world. Imhotep was also the High Priest and famous as a doctor. He was such a man of genious that the Greeks, two thousand years later, deified him under the name of Esculapius.

Now what does Imhotep's invention actually consist of? All he did was to first build a large mastaba and then over it he built a pyramid with four large steps. The pyramid in its final form has six steps on the west part of the mastaba. Centuries later the Sumerians perfected this type of construction in the «ziggurat». Sixty two and a half metres high this pyramid too was originally covered with a facing of smooth stone which today

Detail of a doorway to the «House of the South».

View of the gallery leading to the pyramid of Unas.

Pyramid of Unas.

Detail of the «text of the pyramids», written in the pyramid of Unas.

has completely disappeared. By the side of the pyramid are the remains of what is called the «South House», two fluted columns (strongly reminiscent of Doric columns) unevenly framing a doorway surmounted by a beautiful horizontal frieze bearing a motive of sacred knots to protect it for the future (the Khekern frieze).

To the south of the step pyramid is the pyramid of Unas, the last pharaoh of the Vth dynasty. Of relatively small size, less than 60 metres square, it was already ruined in 2000 B.C. and it is of interest mainly because it contained a large part of the «Pyramid Text», the first collection of magico-religious texts drawn up during the Old Kingdom and destined to protect the dead pharaoh in the Other World. Written in hieroglyphs and painted in green they start in a corridor and extend over the four walls of the special chamber.

The mastaba tombs

As has already been mentioned a mastaba is the tomb of a bobel or dignitary built to resemble the house in which the dead person formerly lived. The Sakkarah necropolis contains a considerable number of mastabas, some of which are among the most renowned for their beauty and the gracefulness of their decoration.

The **Nebet mastaba**, dating from the end of the Vth dynasty, is a typical example because of the rare style of decoration found in the second chamber. This shows the queen herself in the palace harem (the area reserved for the women) where she is witnessing the presentation of offerings while sniffing a flower. The **Visir Unefert's mastaba** on the other hand is VIth dynasty. He is depicted on a wall right at the entrance of the mastaba as an old man walking towards the interior of his sepulchre. The extant decoration in the **Princess Idut's mastaba** is of particular interest. The mastaba contains ten rooms but only five are decorated. One scene shows two seated scribes intent on their work. The artist has been at pains to show the case for their quills,

Mastaba of the visir Unefert.

Mastaba of Nebet.

Bas-reliefs carved into the mastaba ▶ of Princess Idut.

the boxes for the colours and even
the two spare brushes which the
scribe on the left has lodged above
his ear. In the **Kagemmi mastaba**
are to be found tasteful and lively
genre paintings. One quite unusual
scene depicted is of a servant
pouring out bird-seed into an av-
iary while another shows a line of
young girls engaged in an acroba-
tic dance. One the other side of
the necropolis there is the **mastaba
of Ptah-Hotep**, a high functionary
of state, whose tomb is to that of
his son Akhu-Hotep. This mastaba
was discovered by the French archeologist Auguste Mariette who
arrived in Egypt in 1850. The
magnificent bas-reliefs, which can
perhaps be attributed to a certain
Ankgen-Ptah, allow us to see with
a wealth of detail what daily life in
ancient Egypt must have been like.
We can see servants bringing offerings and rowers in a boat
whose gestures and movements resemble those of dancers. The most
complex mastaba is that **of
Mereruka** which was discovered in
1893 and is subdivided into three
parts. It consists in fact of quarters
for the owner, who is also called
Meri or Mera, for his wife the
Princess Uatet-Khethor, who was
also a priestess of Hathor, and for
their children. It was a mastaba
appropriate to the rank of a per-

*Scenes of hunting and dancing in the
mastaba of Kagemmi.*

Two scenes from the mastaba of ▶
Ptah-Hotep.

son who like Mereruka had discharged various public functions during the VIth dynasty. Particularly original in its conception is the scene showing hunting and fishing, in which plants and animals are freely distributed all over the available space in a manner bordering on the fantastic.

The **mastaba of Ti** is perhaps the most beautiful of all. It was already finished in 2600 B.C. when Cheops was preparing to build his great pyramid. Ti, the husband of the Princess Nefr-Hotep, lived during the Vth dynasty. Today we would describe him as a VIP, he was the director of all the Pharaoh's works, his close friend, his confidant, and the man in charge of building the pyramids, or at least this is how he is described in the inscriptions on the tomb. The bas-reliefs in the mastaba are considered to be among the most beautiful examples from the period of the Old Kingdom both because of the high level of artistic expression achieved and for the balance of their composition. Particularly noteworthy is the procession of women elegantly carrying tall baskets on their heads.

Hunting and fishing scenes in the mastaba of Mereruka.

The colossal statue of Ramses II.

MEMPHIS

Memphis is the ancient capital of the 1st «nôme» or province of Lower Egypt, Mennof-Ra, which the Greeks called Memphis and which Herodotus claims was founded by Menes who united the two parts of Egypt. Of Memphis there remains today almost nothing except a few ruins. The prophesy of Jeremiah that «Memphis shall be waste and desolate without an inhabitant» (Jeremiah XLVI, 19) has been well and truly fulfilled. Nevertheless Memphis had known centuries of great splendour culminating in the VIth dynasty when it was the principal centre of the cult of Ptah. In an epigraph found at Abu Simbel Ramses II addressed the god in this manner: «At Memphis I have enlarged your house, I have, built

it with much work, with gold and with precious stones...». Not only this but Memphis was also the site of chariot factories, the main sector in the Egyptian war industry. In the centre of Memphis there must have existed the citadel «with the white walls» started by Imhotep. People of every nationality, of every race and of every religion must have lived and worked in this city.
It is really incredible that of all this great splendour there should be left almost nothing except an unending vista of ruins, truncated colums, walls and bits of stone. With the rise and growth of Alexandria, Memphis was progressively abandoned and fell slowly, but inexorably, into ruins. During the course of excavations, started in the 19th century, the remains of the temple of Ptah, where the pharaohs were crowned, and also

a little chapel in honour of Ptah built by Seti I, were brought to light. In front of the temple there once stood a series of colossal statues of Ramses II, only two of which remain today. One, in red granite, can now be seen in the square by the railway station in Cairo. The second is lying in all its glory on the ground in front of the temple. Originally thirteen metres high, it bears the name of the great pharaoh engraved in his cartouche on the right shoulder, on the breast and on the belt. A few tens of metres from this colossus one finds a sphinx dating perhaps from the era of Amon-Ofis II. Carved from a single block of alabaster it is four and half metres high, eight metres long and weighs, it is believed, at least eighty tonnes and together with others it once flanked the entry to the temple of Ptah.

◄ *The alabaster sphinx portraying Amon-Ofis II.*

The piramid of Mejdum.

◄ *The southern pyramid of Snefru, called the ''rhomboidal pyramid''.*

DAHSHUR

About two kilometres from the Sakkarah necropolis can be found the five pyramids of Dahshur, three built of stone and two of brick and all equally important.

The most northerly one, in brick, is that of Sesostris III (XIIth dynasty) which was once faced with sculpted Tura stone. The most southerly are the pyramids of Amon-Emhat II and Amon-Emhat III. The former, in whose burial chamber was found a splendid collection of jewels, is of stone and the latter is of brick.

The other two pyramids were both constructed by Snefru, the first pharaoh of the IVth dynasty. The length of the sides of the base of the one called the «red pyramid» is more than twice its height (213 metres as against 99 metres). The other one, recognisable from a long way off because of its unusual appearance, is the so-called «rhomboidal pyramid» which is also the best preserved of the necropolis. It owes its name to its odd shape, the slope of the faces changing, a little more than half way up, from 50° to 43°. Another odd feature is that it has two entrances, one to the west and one to the north, which lead to two stepped covered chambers.

MEJDUM

Yet another work of the indefatiguable Snefru, the father of Cheops, is the pyramid at Mejdum, near the Nile at about the level of Fayyum. The Arabs call it «ahram el-kaddah», that is the «false pyramid». In fact rather than a pyramid this highly original construction resembles a large mastaba with sloping sides surmounted by two massive steps. Originally however its appearance must have been quite different with eight large steps terminating in a pointed top. The hypothesis can also be advanced that a start may have been made on an external smooth facing intended to cover the whole thing.

ABYDOS

Today on the west bank of the Nile there stands the village of Arabat el-Madfurnah, literally «Arabat the buried» and the sand has indeed engulfed most of the monuments.

Abydos was the name which the Greeks gave to the ancient city of Thinis, cradle of the oldest dynasties and a holy city dedicated to the cult of Osiris. In fact the myth of Osiris which also emanated from the sanctuary at Busiris (the original name Pa-Uzir means «the dwelling place of Osiris») attained its most perfect realization here in Abydos both as regards the construction of important monuments and as a centre of pilgrimage (all Egyptians had to make a pilgrim-

age to the temple at least once in a life-time). The most important relic of the god, his head, was preserved in the sanctuary of Osiris. According to legend the god Seth killed his brother Osiris, chopped up his body into pieces (thirteen according to some souces, fourty two according to others) and scattered them over the various provinces of Egypt. The goddess Isis, the wife of the dead god, collected all the pieces and placed them in the Osireion in Abydos... all the pieces that is apart from the phallus which was swallowed by a fish in Lake Menzaleh near Port Said. Isis by the force of her love brought her spouse back to life. When he opened his eyes a ray of light was emitted begetting in Isis a son, Horus. The killing of Osiris by his brother Seth is very re-

Portico and façade of the temple of Seti I.

Detail of false door in the ▶
temple of Seti I.

Temple of Seti I: the god Osiris and the goddess Isis. *Temple of Seti I: Pharaoh offers a plumed Zed to the goddess Isis.* ▶

miniscent of the story of Cain and Abel in the Bible.

Of this ancient city where all religious Egyptians longed to have a funerary chapel or at least a commemorative stele, and of the sanctuary, there remain today only a few ruins. On the other hand the palace of Seti I, the Memnonium, famous for its splendid paintings, which was described by Strabonius as an «admirably constructed palace» is extremely well preserved. Excavated by Auguste Mariette the palace was originally built to commemorate the pilgrimage of Seti I to Abydos. Although the work was continued by his son Ramses II the palace was never finished.

The facade of the temple of Hathor.

Bird's-eye view of the Mammisi; details of the hathor ▶
capitals in the temple of Dendera.

DENDERA

Dendera, the Greek name of the city of Tentirys, is a city made holy by the presence of three different sanctuaries, that of Ihy, the sistrum-playing son of Horus, that of Horus himself and that of Hathor. Today the first two have almost totally disappeared, all that remains of Ihy's sanctuary being a monumental door. As far as the third sanctuary is concerned the temple is more or less intact and the numerous other ruins are sufficient to allow us to reconstruct the whole lay-out of this sacred place.

It was dedicated to the goddess Hathor whose name (literally Hat-Hor) means « Horo's dwelling », and who is often depicted as a sacred cow or as a woman whose head is surmounted by a pair of horns.
Built of granite, like most of the temples constructed during the Ptolemaic dynasty, the temple which we so admire today is only the reconstruction of a pre-existing and much older temple which probably went back to the time of Cheops and Pepi I. The temple consists of a splendid hypostyle hall, opening onto the square. It is 25 metres by 42.5 metres and 18 metres high with twenty four hathoric columns, that is columns with a cubic capital bearing the face of the goddess. Inside the temple there was a smaller temple called the « chapel of Holiness », the most hidden and secret spot in the sanctuary. Here the mysteries of the birth of cosmic order from the primeval chaos were celebrated. However Hathor as well as being a cosmic goddess was also the patron of dance and music.
Thus every year at Dendera the popular feast of « drunkenness » was celebrated on the twentieth day of the first month of the flooding.

◄ *Four views of the lively bazaar of Luxor.*

A characteristic carriage in front of the temple of Luxor.

LUXOR

Today it is difficult when one arrives at Luxor to imagine how the great city of Thebes was laid out. For centuries the capital of the Egyptian Kingdom, it was proverbially famous for its wealth («the city where the rich houses are treasures»), it is the city which Homer in the IX canto of the Illiad referred to as «Thebes of the hundred gates». Just a little village during the Memphis era it was the spot where the god of war Montu was worshipped. Its importance started to increase appreciably from the Xth dynasty onwards, for both political and geographical reasons, until finally it became the capital of the pharaohs of the New Kingdom. The god Amon, part of the triad which also included Mut and Khonsu, was worshipped here with great pomp. Every victory and triumph was celebrated by the construction of new and grandiose temples to the god. Its decline started with the sacking of the city by Ashur-ban-pal in 672 B.C. and it was finally destroyed completely by the Ptolemies. In Roman times it was already just a ruin. As with Memphis a prophesy had been fulfilled, «Thebes shall be rent asunder» said Ezechiel (Ezechiel, XXX, 16). The old Egyptian capital is divided in two by a canal; to the south grew up the town of Luxor while to the north the village of Karnak developed.
In Luxor the only witness to its splendid past is the grandiose temple that the Egyptians call

«Amon's southern harem», 260 metres long it was started by Amon-Ofis III, enlarged by Tutmose III and finished by Ramses II. It is joined to the temple of Karnak by a long avenue of sphinxes with ram's heads which the XXth dynasty substituted for the human head. This road has not been completely uncovered and work is still in progress to restore it in its integrity. The road finished at what effectively constituted the entrance of the temple of Luxor, marked by the great pylon built by Ramses II which was 65 metres wide and was decorated with bas-reliefs representing scenes from the military campaign led by Ramses II against the Hittites, and also with the text of the so-called «Poem of Pentaur» in which the Pharaoh's war exploits were celebrated. In front of the pylon there used to stand the two obeliscs of Ramses II but today only one on the left (25 metres high) remains, the other having been carried away to

Seated statue of Ramses II; a view of the mosque from the inner courtyard; Osirian statues between the columns.

◀ *Three views of the pylon of the temple of Amon with the obelisk and the colossi of Ramses II.*

◄ *Two views of the large courtyard of Amon-Ofis III.*

The outside of the temple with round columns; the capitals of the columns represent open papyrus flowers.

France in 1833 and erected by the engineer Lebas on 25th October 1836 in the centre of the Place de la Concorde in Paris. The entrance is flanked by two granite colossi representing the Pharaoh seated on his throne fifteen and a half metres high on a base of about one metre. Originally the two colossi stood beside four huge statues of pink granite having their backs to the pylon, of which one represented the Queen Nefertari and another on the right (which is still standing but is much damaged) represents her daughter Merit-Amon. Beyond this triumphal entrance is

the courtyard of Ramses II in which stand two rows of columns whose capitals represent a closed papyrus flower, with between the columns, Osirian statues. In this courtyard there also stand the little temple of Tutmose III which possesses three chapels dedicated to the triad of Amon, Mut and Khonsu who are worshipped in the sanctuary of Karnak. Finally an imposing colonnade, 25 metres long, leads into the courtyard of Amon-Ofis III which is surrounded on three sides by a sides by a double row of columns with closed papyrus capitals, a veritable pet-

rified forest which is very evocative.

The outside of the temple is also quite interesting. The external wall has numerous doors leading into the various side chapels in which are depicted scenes from the battle against the Syrian-Hittite coalition and also scenes from religious ceremonies. To one side can be found remains of buildings which were part of the Roman camp («castrum» in Latin). The present name of Luxor is derived from the Arabic «El Qousour» a translation of the Latin «castrum».

KARNAK

About three kilometres from the temple at Luxor one finds the vast zone covered by the monuments at Karnak which the Greeks called Hermonthis. The area covered by the monuments is divided into three with rough brick walls separating them. The largest, which covers about thirty hectares, is the central area which is also the best preserved. Diodorus of Sicily said of it that it is the most ancient of the four temples at Thebes. It is the temple dedicated to Amon. On the left is the sanctuary of Montu, the god of war, which is rectangular and covers about two and a half hectares. On the other side covering about nine hectares, of which about half is as yet unexplored, is the sanctuary of the goddess Mut, Amon's wife, who is symbolically represented as a vulture.

The great temple of Amon amazes one by its sheer size. It is the largest temple supported by columns in the world and is so vast that it could easily contain the whole of Notre Dame de Paris and according to Leonard Cottrell «would cover at least half of Manhattan». The most truly amazing feature is the hypostyle hall

These three pictures show the majestic avenue of ram-headed sphinxes leading to the first pylon of the Temple of Karnak.

The colossal statue of Pinedjem in the first courtyard;
the surviving column of the pavilion of Taharka.

The sphinxes of Ramses II in the « Ethiopian ▶
courtyard » and one side of the temple of Ramses III.

which is one hundred and two metres long by fifty
three metres wide and in which there stand (this time
one is really tempted to say defying the centuries!)
one hundred and thirty four columns 23 metres high.
The tops of the open papyrus shaped capitals have a
circumference of about fifteen metres and are big
enough for fifty people to stand on them. A veritable
«forest of columns» which excite tremendous emo-
tion because of their size and the play of light and
shade on them. During the XIXth dynasty 81,322
persons worked in the temple of Amon if we count
not only the priests and guardians but also the workmen and peasants involved. The temple enjoyed the
income from a considerable number of estates, mar-
kets and work sites to which one should add all the
riches and booty which the Pharaoh brought back
from his victorious military expeditions. Various
pharaohs contributed to the realization of the hypostyle hall. Amon-Ofis III built the twelve columns in
the central nave which support the enormous architraves. Ramses I initiated the decoration and this work
was continued by Seti I and Ramses II.
Beyond the hypostyle hall there once stood (today

A few details of the hypostyle hall.

only one remains) the obeliscs of Tutmose I which were 23 metres high and weighed 143 tonnes. Higher still is the one erected by his daughter Hatshepsut for the construction of which it is said that the queen spared no expense, the chronicles of the period state that she provided « bushels of gold as if they were sacks of grain » for the project. What then temains to be said about the « Banqueting Hall », Tutmose III's Akh-Menu? Here too there is a beautiful hypostyle hall with two rows of ten columns and one row of thirty two rectangular pillars. From the traces of paint-

The obelisk of Tutmose I, the statues of two pharaohs
and the gigantic scarab on the northwest corner of the
sacred lake, perhaps originally in the mortuary temple
of Amon-Ofis III.

Bird's-eye view of the sacred lake with the hypostyle ►
hall in the background. Below, part of an obelisk of
Amon-Ofis III.

ings dating from the 6th century A.D. we know that
this hall was converted into a church by some Christian monks.

The complex at Karnak also had a sacred lake, 120
metres long, where according to Herodotus the priests
carried out their nocturnal rituals. Today the reflec-
tion of the imposing remains of the temple can be seen
in the lake, and on those nights when the monuments
are illuminated for the inevitable « Son et Lumière »,
the ancient splendour of Thebes comes back to life.

Fragments of wall, called « talatat », from the Palace of Akhen-Aton; the goddess Hathor, from the tomb of Tutankhamon.

THE LUXOR MUSEUM

Although of recent institution the Luxor Museum contains many interesting exhibits. The most curious item is the reconstruction of a wall, 18 metres long, from the temple that Akhen-Aton built in Thebes. The two hundred and eighty three blocks of which it is made up were found in the filling of the ninth pylon of the temple of Amon at karnak. The wall, consisting of hundreds of small scenes, depicts, among other things, work in the fields and in artisans' workshops and the Paraoh and Queen Nefertiti worshipping the sun. In a showcase at the entrance to the museum there is a most elegant bull's head in gilded wood.

THE COLOSSI OF MEMNON

In the immense plain around Thebes between the Nile and the Valley of the Kings, one can still admire what remains of the monumental avenue which used to lead to the temple of Amon-Ofis III. The temple has unfortunately disappeared and what remains are commonly referred to as the «colossi of Memnon». These two gigantic statues, 20 metres high with feet 2 metres long and 1 metre thick, were cut out of single blocks of sandstone and represent Pharaoh seated on his throne with his hands on his knees. The more southerly colossus, although appreciably damaged, has suffered less than the other one. Certain legends have become attached to the latter. It would seem that in

The « Colossi of Memnon ».

the year 27 B.C. an earthquake which shook all the monuments at Thebes split open this enormous block of stone and the upper half, down to the waist, fell to the ground. However some historians attribute this damage to the vandalism of Cambyses, which seems more likely as Egypt has never been a country prone to earthquakes.

It was observed that every morning at sunrise the remains of the statue gave out an indefinite and prolonged sound and some travellers believed that they heard a sad but harmonious song. The Greek poets quickly grafted a legend, not lacking in charm, into this strange story which was attested to by the great historians such as Strabonius, Pausanias, Tacitus, Lucianus and Philostrates. The « singing stone » they said represented Memnon, the mythical son of Aurora and Tithon, and king of Egypt and Ethiopia. Sent by his father to the aid of Troy besieged by the Greeks he covered himself in glory by killing Antiloques, son of Nestor, but in his turn be succombed to the vengeful hand of Achilles. The tearful Aurora beseeched the powerful Jupiter to resuscitate her son at least once a day. Thus it is that each morning while Aurora caressed her son with her rays, he replied to his unconsolable mother by emitting a long plaintive cry...

In spite of the poetic charm of this legend the phenomenon had thoroughly natural causes. The sounds emitted were due to the vibrations produced at the broken surface by the sudden transition from the cold of the night resulting from the heat generated by the first rays of the sun. History seems moreover to justify this scientific explanation. In fact no author before Strabonius mentions the « singing » of the Memnon colossus, while those who do lived between the date when the statue was broken and its restoration by Septimus Severus (193-221 A.D.). Engraved on the legs of the colossus are to be found numerous and in some cases very odd inscriptions added over the course of the centuries. One of them is conceived in these terms: « Take note, Oh Theis, thou who reignest over the waters, that Memnon still lives and, warmed by the maternal flame, he lifts up his sonorous voice at the foot of the Libyan mountains in Egypt at the point where the Nile divides Thebes of the beautiful gates in two; while, thou Achilles, formerly so insatiable for battle, art now silent both on the fields of Troy and on the mountains of Thessaly ».

The temple of Medinet Habu.

Osirian pillars in the inner courtyard, the statues of two ▶
gods and the lion-headed goddess Sekhmet.

MEDINET HABU

For a long time Medinet Habu was nothing more than a very rich quarry from which large squared blocks of stone could be obtained. In the Christian era a village grew up here which the Copts called Djeme and which occupied a large part of the zone where the temple used to be. In fact this new use of the area preserved many remains which might otherwise have been lost. The excavations brought to light traces of a whole city which extended around the Pharaoh's palace, but only a single house has been uncovered in recognizable form, that of an inspector of the necropoli.

The complex at Medinet Habu consisted of the temple of Ramses III in front of which stood the little temple of Tutmose I and the chapels of the deities who worshipped Amon. The beautiful South Gate, known as the Royal Pavilion, which is set between a pair of towers and above which there are two rows of longitudinal windows is of imposing almost militaristic appearance. Even the bas-reliefs on the walls of the towers underline the «war-like» character of this building showing as they do the sacrifice of prisoners, the Pharaoh bringing enemy captives before the god Amon, etc...

The temple of Ramses III is stylistically one of the most perfect buildings which Egyptian architecture has left us. Beyond the pylon which is 63 metres high and decorated with war scenes, one enters

a first courtyard one side of which is taken up with a gallery having Osirian pillars. Beyond other pylons and other courtyards one eventually arrives at the last hypostyle hall which is dominated by a group of statues depicting Ramses III with the god Thot. Not all the decoration in the temple of Medinet Habu is militaristic. For example on one of the architraves the goddess Nekhbet, depicted as a vulture, protects Upper Egypt and, symbolically, the whole temple.

THE RAMESSEUM

The Ramesseum is the name which was given in the last century to the temple complex built by Ramses II between the desert and the village of Gurnah. Diodorus of Sicily himself was amazed at the complexity and architectonic grandeur of the monument. Unfortunately today only a few ruins remain. On the façade of the hypostyle hall one can still see the pillars with, abutting into them, statues of the pharaoh in the guise of Osiris (for this reason they are called Osiriac pillars) and, lying there like a fallen giant, the remains of the syenite statue of Ramses II sitting on his throne. It is believed that this statue must have been at least 17 metres high and have weighed more than a thousand tonnes.

The decoration of the temple again shows the exploits of the pharaoh who stopped the Hittite advance. However there are also scenes depicting the festivities held in the first month of summer to honour Min, the prehistoric god of fertility, in whose honour the Pharaoh had to sacrifice a white bull. Another unusual and interesting decoration is that on one of the walls of the hypostyle hall. The sons and daughters of Ramses are shown in two files lined up according to the order of succession. In eighteenth position is Mineptah who in fact succeeded Ramses II on the Egyptian throne.

General view of the Osirian pillars in the hypostyle hall and the remains of the colossus.

The mortuary temple of Ramses II, or Ramesseum.

THE VALLEY OF THE KINGS

On the mountain-side behind Thebes there are many small valleys of which the Valley of the Kings, also known as «the tombs of the king of Biban el-Muluk» is the most famous.

Originally it appeared as a gorge lost among the rocky ravines. Today even though roads have been built making access much easier, it still retains intact its mysterious fascination. Its history began with the unlikely decision of a pharaoh, Tutmose I, not only to build his tomb away from the funerary temple but to ensure his body burial not in a monument but in a secret place. His resolution to do this broke a tradition going back 1700 years. The architect, Ineni, excavated for the sovereign a well-like tomb in an isolated valley and then carved out of the rock a steep stairway leading down to the burial chamber, thus setting a precedent which was followed by all successive pharaohs.

Tutmose I's rest however did not last long, neither did that of the other kings. The history of the Valley of the Kings is one long story of pillaging, plundering and night time robberies by the light of a few torches. It was not only thieves, who already during the pharaonic era were engaged in systematic plundering to obtain the jewels and other treasures, but also religious and devout men who, knowing that their sovereigns were not safe, carried them away from one burial spot to bury them in another. And so it went on; Ramses III was buried three times!

Almost all the inhabitants of the village of Gurnah made a living from this commerce of objects stolen from the tombs, the plundering of tombs having for all practical purposes become a regular occupation which from the XIIIth century B.C. onwards was passed down from father to son. The family of Abdul Rasul was the guardian of a great secret: the sarcophagi of thirty six pharaohs were gathered together in a single isolated anonymous burial place. The secret came to light in 1881 after a long interrogation of a member of the family. The Deputy Director of the Cairo Museum, Emil Brugsch-Bey, was then taken to the mouth of the pit. It is hard to imagine what this scholar must have felt when the light of the torch revealed the mortal remains of the great pharaohs of the ancient world all jumbled together higgledy-piggledy. Before him lay Amosis I, Amon-Ofis I, Tutmose III and Ramses II (Ramses the Great)...

A week later two hundred men packed up the mummies and carried them down the valley to the point where a boat was waiting to transport them to the Cairo Museum. And now something

Above: entrance to the tombs of Ramses VI and of Tutankhamon; below, the road leading into the Valley: dominating the background is the «Theban crown».

strange and very moving happened. On learning that the rediscovered pharaohs were about to leave their age-old burial spot, the peasants and their wives gathered on the banks of the river and as the boat slowly passed by they paid homage to their ancient kings, the men by discharging their rifles in the air, the women by raising their voices in lament and scattering ashes over their faces.

Tomb of Ramses IX

Although considerably damaged this tomb is interesting for the pictures of scenes from the «Book of the Dead», the «Litanies of the Sun» and from the «Book of things which are in the Duat».

At right: the sun barge of Khnum, with the gods Hathor and Horus.

Below: two guardian genii, the serpent and the scarabeus.

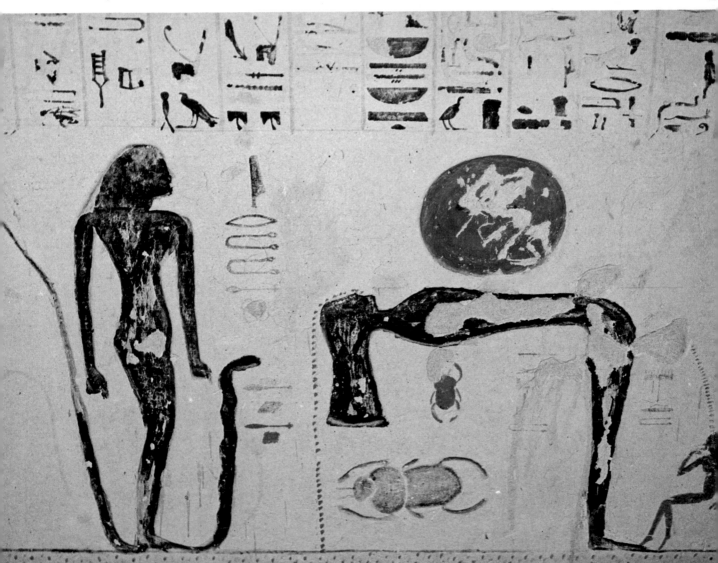

The tomb of Tutankhamon.

The golden mask of Tutankhamon now in the Egyptian ► Museum in Cairo.

Tomb of Ramses VI

This very small tomb has a magnificent ceiling showing two celestial hemispheres with the stellar gods in procession behind the solar barges sailing down the celestial Nile.

Tomb of Tutankhamon

The story of the discovery of the tomb of this pharaoh who died when he was barely eighteen years old is too long, too fascinating and too mysterious to be told in its entirety here.
It was discovered on 4th November 1922 by Howard Carter (acting on behalf of Lord Carnavon) and it made history because of the enormous amount of treasure found in the burial chamber which, fortunately had remained

untouched by grave robbers. It is still worthwhile to read Carter's own account of this historic discovery in order to relive day by day, moment by moment its various phases.
Unlike its contents the tomb itself was very modest, perhaps because it was built in great haste as a result of the unexpected death of the king. Inside among all the funeral trimmings the thing which stands out because of its great beauty is the pharaoh's sarcophagus. It is more correct to say the sacrophagi since the royal corpse was contained in three mummy cases: the first of gilded wood, the second also of gilded wood but with the addition of a powdered glass paste while the third is of solid gold. The golden sarcophagus is one of the greatest masterpieces of the goldsmiths' art of all time; it contains two hundred kilos of gold, is one and half metres high and is

encrusted with lapislazzuli, turquoises and cornelians.
However among all this glitter the thing which made the greatest impression on Carter and his party was a little wreath of dried up flowers, a last pathetic gesture from the consort of the boy-pharaoh. Finally let us not forget that in addition to the already romantic story of the discovery itself there is that obscure business that has come to be known as «the Pharaoh's curse». The sudden violent deaths of the majority of those who took part in Lord Carnavon's expedition, with the exception, strange to say, of Carter himself, lent strength to the belief in a posthumous vendetta by the dead Pharaoh whose eternal sleep had been disturbed.
History of course is full of such legends and this one only adds to the fascination of the already fascinating romance of Tutankhamon.

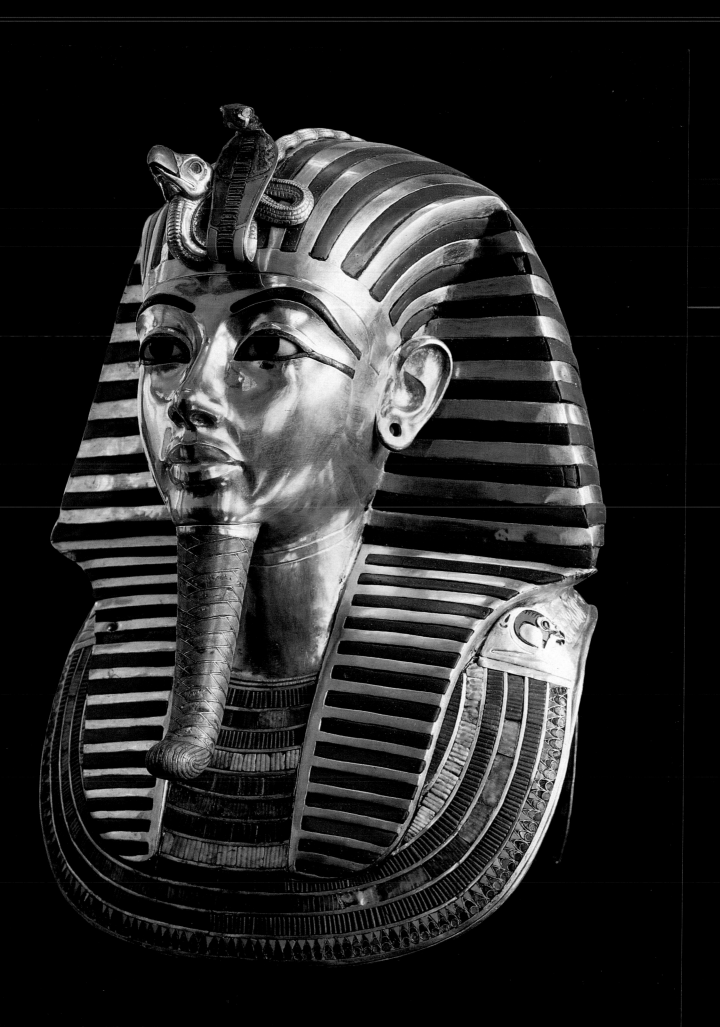

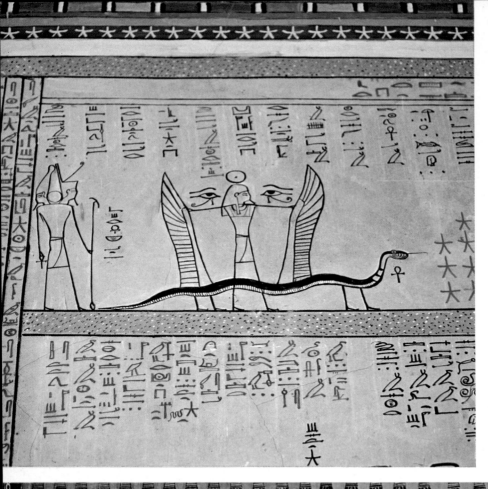

Tomb of Amon-Ofis II

The tomb of Amon-Ofis II is situated at the feet of a rocky spur. A long corridor with steep steps leads to the hypogeum which after making a right angle turn opens out into a vast hall whose roof is supported by six magnificently decorated rectangular pillars. It was in this chamber that the sovereign's sarcophagus was found. The mummy was intact including a garland of flowers round the neck and a small bunch of mimosa laid over the heart. Along the walls of the hall, looking just like a long payrus which has been unwound, are depicted scenes from the «Book of things which are in the Duat».

At left: at far left, the two-faced Pharaoh wearing the crown of Upper and Lower Egypt, preceded by the solar serpent.

Below: divinities, canopic jars and other symbols of resurrection.

On the right, the sarcophagus chamber, its wall decorated with scenes from the Book of the Amduat.

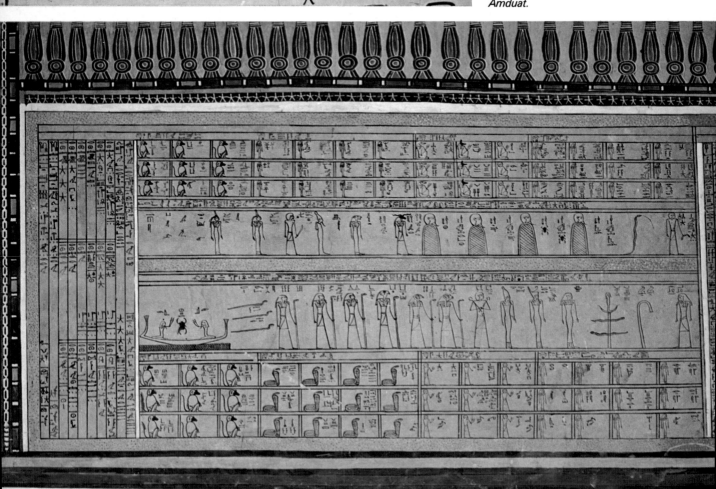

Tomb of Tutmose III

Of difficult access, this tomb contains paintings which, for their concise graphic style, are considered among the most beautiful in all the Valley of the Kings. An extremely original and important sovereign, this Tutmose III. Illegitimate son of Tutmose II, nominated Pharaoh at the death of his father while still very young, he was dethroned by his aunt Hatshepsut, who had herself proclaimed regent. Tutmose III then gave himself over to a posthumous personal revenge, systematically cancelling the name of the queen from all monuments and replacing it with his own name or that of his father.

This king's military expeditions have remained famous, especially the eight campaigns against the Mitanns. Voyaging by sea to Phenicia, where they disembarked, his army traversed Syria, carrying with them through the desert the ships on which to cross the Euphrates River. Finally meeting in battle the hostile population, Tutmose was victorious, pursuing the defeated enemy at length.

Tomb of Seti I

By the complexity of its construction the tomb of Seti I is one of the most noteworthy in the Theban necropolis. It contains numerous flights of stairs and galleries leading to rooms supported by pillars. In one of these Giovanni Battista Belzoni discovered the pharaoh's sarcophagus which is carved out of a single massive block of alabaster. The mummy was not there, it had already been carried away together with others to an unknown common grave.

At right: the barge of the god Khnum and the serpent which protects the tabernacle of the ram-headed god.

Below: representations of the world in the Duat, with the serpent Apofis, and of the reign of Osiris, with a procession of genii and gods. The two kingdoms are separated by a long wall in which open doors protected by guardians.

◀ *At left: detail of the seven hundred and forty guardian divinities.*

◀ *Below, the funeral chamber and sarcophagus.*

THE VALLEY OF THE QUEENS

About a kilometre and a half from the Valley of the Kings is the Valley of the Queens which today is called «Biban el-Harim». In the region, eighty tombs have been discovered there but they are badly damaged, some showing traces of fire, others having been used as stables.

The tombs mostly date from the period 1300 to 1100 B.C., that is from the XIXth and XXth dynasties. A little more open than the Valley of the Kings, access is via a pass where stelae commemorating some of the achievement of Ramses III can be seen. Prayers addressed to Osiris and Anubis have been carved on some of the rocks.

Tomb of Queen Thiti

At one time used as a stable for asses the tomb of Queen Thiti, who may have been the wife of one of the pharaohs of the XXth dynasty, contains some beautiful paintings in delicate shades of pink.

Tomb of Prince Amon-her-Khopechef

(It should be noted that those of the pharaohs' offspring who died in childhood were also buried in the Valley of the Queens). The decoration in this tomb intended for the son of Ramses III is exceptional both for the brilliance and the intensity of the colour which is dominated by a magnificent ultramarine blue. In the first room we see the Pharaoh presenting his son to various gods, Thot, Ptah and the four sons of Horus (Hapi, Amset, Duamutef and Kebensenuf). The latter four gods after taking part in the rite of mummification of Osiris with Anubis became the patrons of the canopic jars.

Below: the Queen, wearing a high plumed headdress, her body outlined in a flowing, semi-transparent garment, presents offerings to the four genii of the after-life.

Above right: frieze on architrave with winged solar disk flanked by cobras.

Below right: Prince Amon-her-Khopechef and the ram-headed god Arietes.

Representation of Ramses III with the goddess Isis and the Pharaoh's young son who died during an epidemic in the Palace of Thebes.

Ramses III introduces his son to the world of the After-life, presenting him to Ptah, the god of death (above) and to Thot, the dog-headed god gatekeeper of the Underworld (below).

Tomb of Prince Pra-her-Umenef

Pra-her-Umenef was another of the sons of Ramses III who died rather young and who like his brothers is buried in this valley. The decoration is more or less the same as in the other tombs and shows the dead prince being presented by his father to various divinities. The dominant colours however are yellow ochre and pink in this case.

Above left: three guardians armed with long knives stand watch at the doors of the world of the Duat. Recognizable are, at right, the goddess Nekhbet, protectress of Upper Egypt, in the form of a vulture; next to her, the god Sobek with the head of a crocodile and lastly, far left, another guardian viewed from the front (very rare in Egyptian iconography where the profile is practically obligatory)

Below left: three dog-headed animals, called «guardians of dawn» stand watch at the entrance to the World of the Duat. The figure standing erect is armed with a long knife.

At right: representation of the goddess Isis, protectress of the dead.

Overall view of funerary complex.

DEIR EL-BAHARI

One thousand two hundred years after Imhotep another architect, Senmut, won himself a place in Egyptian history by designing another architectural masterpiece. Queen Hatshepsut who was more of a patron of the arts than a military commander, ordered a funerary monument to be built for her father Tutmose I and herself, choosing for the site a valley which had already been consecrated to the goddess Hathor but had then been abandoned. The great insight of her architect-minister was the way in which he exploited the rocks spread out in a fan shape behind the monument. The conception of the monument was thus new, indeed revolutionary. The temple, pointing to the east, consisted of a series of vast terraces which by means of ramps led to the sanctuary. Access to the first terrace was by means of an avenue lined with sphinxes and obeliscs. At the end of this terrace was a portico from which a ramp led to the second terrace which was also closed at the end by a portico. On one of the walls a series of beautiful bas-reliefs depicts the birth and childhood of the queen as well as the expedition she organised to the mysterious country of Punt which has been assumed to be somewhere in the centre of Africa since among the things depicted are giraffes, monkeys, panther skins and ivory objects. The left hand side of the valley on the other hand was oc-

cupied by the gigantic funerary temple of Montu-Hotep I who, five hundred years before Hatshepsut, had also had the idea of building his temple in the valley. He built his tomb according to ideas some of which were typical of the Old Kingdom while others foreshadowed the New Kingdom. At a later period a Christian convent installed itself in Queen Hatshepsut's monument. This was called the «northern convent» which gave the area its present name of Deir el-Bahari. We should be thankful that the convent was installed in the temple because it protected it from later depredations.

Details of the temple of Deir el-Bahari with the frescoed walls inside the colonnade.

VALLEY OF THE NOBLES

The tombs of the great dignitaries from the dynasties of the Middle Kingdom are to be found in three adjoining areas, Assassif, Khokhah and Sheik Abd el-Gurnah. Their main characteristics are extreme architectural simplicity compared with the royal tombs and a choice of iconography notable for its freshness and vitality. Furthermore the tombs in this valley furnish valuable information on court life in ancient Egypt such as the offices and functions of the various dignitaries.

Rakh-Mara's Tomb

This tomb, one of the biggest of the XVIIIth dynasty, belonged to Rakh-Mara who was governor of the city and visir under both Tutmose III and Amon-Ofis II. The most interesting scenes are those showing the arrival of tribute from foreign countries. Thus there are shown the envoys from Punt, from Kefti (which can perhaps be identified with Crete), and those from Ratenu who are northern Assyrians and Syrians, and finally black envoys from Kush.

At left: above, workmen sculpt a statue of the Pharaoh; below, bearers and custodians of the funerary furnishings.

Kiki's Tomb

The «royal superintendent» Kiki was buried in this tomb which later was used as a stable. On one of the walls is depicted the journey of the dead man's remains to Abydos and one can see the professional mourners wailing as well as servants carrying offerings.

Representation of Kiki, with beard, followed by his bride who holds a sistrum. In the upper panel, the husband and wife worship Anubis.

Menna's Tomb

The owner of this tomb, described as the «Scribe of the Land Register of the Master of Upper and Lower Egypt», utilized a pre-existing tomb and enlarged it. The decoration depicts scenes (such as work in the fields, the pilgrimage to Abydos, the sons and daughters of Menna) which are among the most elegant in the whole necropolis.

Above left: banquet scene with a handmaiden pouring out perfumed oils while the wife's arm affectionately encircles her husband's shoulders. On their heads the couple wear highly original perfume holders formed of empty gourds filled with a scented creme sending out its fragrance as it dissolves with the heat.

Scene of slaughter and purification of a bull to be offered as sacrifice.

Sennefer's Tomb

This tomb is reached via a stair with 43 steps which goes down into the rock. Sennefer was the Prince of the Southern City during the reign of Amon-Ofis II. The tomb is famous for the beautiful bower of grapes painted on the ceiling of the vestibule.

At right: Sennefer and his wife, Seth-Nefer, sail the Nile seated beneath a canopy while a servant presents a richly prepared table.

Below right: two Anubis stand guard at the doors of the After-life; between them, a tall vase of flowers.

Ramosis's Tomb

Ramosis had the title «Governor of the City and Viceroy» under the heretical pharaoh Akhen-Aton. At the death of his sovereign Ramosis had to abandon the tomb which he had started building, which must have been at Tell el-Amarna although no trace of it has yet been found, and build another at Thebes. The bas-reliefs are particularly beautiful both for their plastic qualities and for the naturalness, especially of the human face.

At left: two examples of basso rilievi representing Ramosis alone and with his wife Satamon.

Above right: a cortege of servants bears the furnishings; recognisable are a bed with headrest, four chests, a chair.

Below right: procession of flower bearers.

VALLEY OF THE WORKMEN

Today the name Deir el-Medina is used to indicate the valley with the village and necropolis of all the workmen who built and decorated the royal tombs of Thebes.

These were the stonecutters, masons, painters and sculptors who every day made their way to the royal necropolis through a path leading over the hills of Deir el-Bahari. The women remained in the village, cultivating the wheat and barley. The teams of workmen were directed by overseers (architects or artists of various kinds). The painters were divided into two groups: those who worked on the right-hand walls and those who worked on the left-hand walls. The houses of these workers were extremely simple dwellings. Built of dried brick, whitewashed inside, they were very small with a tiny entrance hall, one room and a kitchen. Sometimes, but not often, they had a cellar and a terrace.

Tomb of Inherkha

At the time of Ramses III and Ramses IV, Inherkha was «Deputy Master of the Two Egypts in the Place of Truth». He had two tombs built at the same time. The one lower down the valley, nearer to the village, shows vivid fantasy and great inventive capacity, especially in the scenes illustrating family life, such as the one where a husband and wife, dressed alike in linen garments, are shown affectionately seated together at a banquet.

Tomb of Sennedjen

The main chamber is all that remains today of the tomb of Sennedjen, an official at the time of the XIX Dynasty and «Servant in the Square of Truth». The paintings found here are, for their liveliness and freshness of colour, among the most beautiful of the entire valley. On one end wall is painted Sennedjen, who, accompanied by his bride, works in the Fields of Ialu (the Egyptian paradise), plowing, sowing and harvesting grain. On the other end wall (below) the husband and wife worship the gods in the After-life. At the head of all the other gods is Osiris who, with his green skin, symbolizes the renewal of life at springtime.

Above: a scarabeus with «Hathor's necklace» and, below, the elegant stride of four exquisitely refined Anubis.

A camel with a load of sugar cane, a typical dwelling
along a canal; the tourist river boats anchored on the
Nile and a typical felucca.

ESNA

In ancient times this was the capital of the IIIrd nôme or province of Upper Egypt. It was called «Latopolis» by the Greeks because of the worship of a sacred fish, Lato, which was the object of a special cult and of which numerous mummified examples have been found.

The present village only contains a temple dedicated to the god Khnum which is a Ptolemaic restoration of a pre-existing XVIIIth dynasty temple. The hypostyle hall, which is 33 metres by 18 and contains twenty four columns 13.5 metres high, is more or less intact. The capitals of the columns are the most interesting feature thanks to the various sculpted floral motifs.

The great entrance pylon to the temple.

◄ *Detail of the capitals in the inner hall of the temple of Khnum at Esna and a general view of the facade.*

EDFU

Edfu's main claim to fame in Egyptian history is that in this other-wise unimportant small town there is the best preserved temple in the whole of Egypt. The ancient capital of the IInd nôme of Upper Egypt, it was called Apollinopolis Magna by the Greeks.

The temple, which is dedicated to Horus, was built during the Ptolemaic period on top of an older temple dating from the time of Tutmose III. Because of its imposing dimensions it is considered the most important after Karnak. It is 137 metres long and the front is 79 metres wide. It has a pylon 36 metres high. On guard at the entrance to the temple are two very beautiful black granite statues depicting Horus in the form of a falcon. The name of the god in fact derives from the word «hr» which means hawk. Behind the two statues stand the external walls of the temple together with massive figure of Horus and Hathor. The wide grooves either side of the doorway once housed the flag masts from which fluttered their standards. Inside the sancturary, still in a perfect state of preservation, is a very beautiful tabernacle carved from a single block of grey granite and which stands about 4 metres high. The inscriptions tell us that it was constructed under Nectanebus II (360 B.C.).

Before entering the temple it is interesting to look at the «mammisi» constructed under Evergete II. In the Coptic language «mammisi» means «the place of childbirth» and refers to the spot where symbolically Horus is re-born every day. It is for this reason that it has become sacred to those in child-birth and to all women who want to have a child.

Three pictures of the ''large courtyard of libations''; the columns are joined at mid-height by intercolumn-walls; note the majestic black granite statue of Horus.

KOM OMBO

Situated between Edfu and Aswan, Kom Ombo is the ancient city of Pa-Sebek, that is the «home of Sebek» the crocodile god who was already worshipped in predynastic times. In Kom Ombo is to be found the impressive remains of a temple of somewhat unusual style. In fact it is a double temple obtained by joining two temples along one side. The right-hand temple is the one consecrated to the god Sebek, the god of fertility who is also believed to be the creator of the world, while the left-hand temple is dedicated to the god Haroeris, that is «Horus the Great» the solar god of war. This temple was also rebuilt by the Ptolemies who adapted a temple built at the time of Tutmose III. The two temples were surrounded by a large outer wall which opened into the Nile via two gateways. In the hypostyle hall there are three rows of columns, one of which runs down the centre dividing it into two separate sanctuaries in a rather original manner. Then come the sanctuaries clearly separated by a space.

Two images of the temple of Kom Ombo.

A panoramic view of Aswan, with white feluccas floating down the Nile.

ASWAN

The present town of Aswan is built on the site of the old market of the city of Abu, which the Greeks called Elefantina, and which means «elephant island». Capital of the Ist nôme or province of Upper Egypt its former name was Syene. The red granite, syenite, which was used in religious building, for obeliscs, for colossi, for the temples themselves, was extracted from its numerous wealthy quarries. The quarries were still being used in Roman times when the poet Juvenal was exiled to Syene by Tiberius. Another curiosity of the area is a well whose vertical sides are only illuminated by the rays of the sun on the day of the summer solstice because of its proximity to the Tropic of Cancer. Eratostenes, the

writer, took it as the point of departure for the measurement of the circumference of the earth.
On the west bank of the Nile cut into the hill called Tabet el-Haua (the «windy peak») can be found a necropolis containing about fourty tombs going back to the IIIrd millenium N.C. By means of steep narrow stairways one can climb up to the various hypogea, small funerary chapels many of which still have their terraces, colonnades, doors and windows. The tombs then, situated one above the other, give the impression of a rocky city. Many of the hypogea were destroyed and burnt during the Christian era by the Copts. They erected a fortified monastery on the top of the hill and this in its turn was destroyed during an incursion by Saladin's army. Also to be found in this area is the

famous **mausoleum of the Aga Khan** who died in 1957.
It is now necessary to talk about the celebrated Aswan Dam, Egypt's «protection against hunger». The project was entrusted to the Soviet Union and construction was started in January 1960. On the 14th May 1964 the waters of the Nile were released into the derivation canal. The construction of this dam with the consequent formation of an artificial lake, lake Nasser, 500 kilometres long with a capacity of 157 thousand million cubic metres making it the world's second largest after the one on the Zambesi, has resolved quite a few of Egypt's economic problems. Egypt's problems can be summed up in two figures. Of a surface area of 900,000 square kilometres only 38,000 were previously under

The mausoleum of the Aga Khan; the monastery of St. Simeon; feluccas on the Nile with the necropolis of the Princes in the background and the outside of the Aswan museum.

cultivation, that is about 4%. With the dam not only would it be possible to increase the area under cultivation but an ambitious system of irrigation would be set up and the annual production of electrical energy would be increased. On the other hand monuments of priceless historical and artistic value in the area covered by the lake would have been lost. The whole world waited with bated breath while an incredible salvage operation enabled the dam to be built without the total loss of so much of the country's artistic and cultural patrimony.

The Tomb of Siremput I

Of this tomb, which belonged to the son of Zat-Seni, a prince of the XIIth dynasty, there unfortu-

nately remains today very little to bear witness to the fact that it was the biggest and the most richly decorated in the whole necropolis. One can still see part of the surrounding wall and the limestone doorway at the entrance which has delicate bas-reliefs showing scenes from the life of the dead prince. At the end, the façade of the tomb had a portico with six pillars.

The Tomb of Siremput II

Siremput II was the «Hereditary Prince» during the reign of the XIIth dynasty pharaoh Amon-Emhat II. The hypogeum consists of an initial chamber with six pillars, a gallery flanked by six niches each with a mummy-shaped statue of the dead prince, a second

square chamber with four pillars, each one decorated with a splendid picture of Siremput, and finally a frescoed chapel. In the latter is a scene showing the prince with his small son paying homage to him in front of a table laid for a meal with bread, sweets, fruit including bunches of grapes and even a duck. Beneath the table stand carafes of wine. The adjacent wall shows the prince's wife, a priestess of Hathor, who is also seated before a ritual meal.

Chapel of the tomb of Siremput II. ▶

Entrance to the tomb of Prince Siremput I.

Granite Quarries

The old granite quarries about two kilometres from the city stretch along the Nile for about six kilometres. From the grooves which have been cut in a regular manner into the syenite walls we can get some idea of how the blocks of granite were removed. Wedges of wood were inserted into these grooves, which indicated the surface to be cut out, and then moistened. The expansion of the wood caused the stone to split along the desired directions and in this way fairly smooth surfaces were obtained which were ready for polishing. Nearby can be seen the famous «unfinished obelisc» which would have been about 41 metres high with a weight of about 1267 tonnes. It was to have been erected for

The unfinished obelisk of Queen Hatshepsut and an aerial view of the first cataract of the Nile.

Queen Hatshepsut but fissures developed in several points and it was never removed from the rock.

The Island of Sehel

A few kilometres from Aswan can be found the first cataract on the Nile, a vast area of turbulent water and eddying whirlpools broken by numerous outcrops of rock and little islands. The island of Sehel in the midst of this minuscule archipelago of islands is well worth visiting. Gigantic blocks of granite covered with figures and inscriptions can be seen lying around without any semblance of order. The oldest date from the VIth dynasty but there are examples of all periods up to the Ptolemaic period. The graffiti commemorate the passage of various royal dignitaries.

Stele n. 81 on the island of Sehel, also known as the "stele of famine".

The Temple of Kalabsha with the High Dam monument.

PHILAE

In the midst of an evocative panorama of granitic rocks, the columns and pillars of this island sacred to the goddess Isis rise up towards a cloudless sky, creating the impression that one is in one of those landscapes which exist only in the imagination. The temple of Philae has one of the three best preserved Ptolemaic temples, the other two being those of Edfu and Dendera.

Following the construction of the old dam on the first cataract in 1904, the temple found itself under water for the greater part of the year and it was only during August that it was visitable because it was only during this period that all the sluice gates were open in order to relieve the pressure due to the flooding of the Nile. After the construction of the big dam at Aswan it became necessary in order to save the temple, to dismantle it, move it to

The left side of the Temple of Isis with the first and second pylons, an air view of the island of Agilkia and the facade of the first pylon.

Looking down on the second pylon and a detail of the bas-reliefs; a detail of the Pavillion of Nectanebo I with its bell-shaped columns and Hathorian columns; the elegant Pavillion of Trajan.

the island of Egelika, 150 metres to the north, and then put it up again.

The cult of Isis at Philae goes back a very long way and there was a tradition that at least once in his life every Egyptian should go on a pilgrimage to the sacred island. Philae is the smallest of the three islands at the end of the group of rocks which form the first cataract and it is about 400 metres long and 135 metres wide. The southern part of the island is occupied by the complex of monuments which form the sanctuary dedicated to the goddess. It was maintained that the miraculous and be-

neficial flooding of the Nile each year had its origin there. After Justinian completed the task of evangelizing Nubia, the bishop Teodorus in 535 A.D. converted the temple into a church dedicated to St. Stephen. The southern extremity of the island is occupied by the pavilion of Nectanebo I, a building with fourteen Hathoric columns. This same Pharaoh initiated the construction of the first pylon of the temple of Isis which is decorated at the bottom with the famous scene in which the pharaoh Ptolemy XIII is offering prisoners of war as a sacrifice to Hator and Horus.

The facade of the Large Temple of Abu Simbel and two statues on the right.

ABU SIMBEL

Three hundred and twenty kilometres from Aswan in Nubia is to be found Abu Simbel the most beautiful and imaginative construction of the greatest and most whimsical pharaoh in Egyptian history. This temple is dedicated in theory to Amon-Ra, Harmakis and Ptah but in practice it was constructed for the greater glory of its builder, Ramses the Great (Ramses II).
To the Pharaoh's architects the temple represented a tremendous challenge which, two thousand years later, was to be taken up

again by the engineers of the world community in order to save it from the waters of the Nile. In this lonely place lost in the middle of the Nubian desert the temple, which is 38 metres wide by 65 metres long, had been carved out of a single piece of rock. The unusual façade was carved by a «multitude of workmen whose swords had led them to prison» working under the direction of the chief mason. The façade consists of four colossal statues of the Pharaoh seated on his throne. Each statue is twenty metres high, measures four metres from ear to ear and one metre along the line of the lips. The statues are not only symbols of the attributes of Ramses but are also functional be-

ing the columns which support the façade, some 31 metres high. The work of the stone-cutters and sculptors was followed by that of the painters which at the time of its execution was remarkable for its wide range of colour but which unfortunately has been completely destroyed by the passage of time. Penetrating into the heart of the mountain one reaches the sanctuary where formerly there stood statues of the triad to whom the temple was dedicated together with one of Ramses himself. It was here that what was called the «miracle of the sun» took place. Twice a year, on 21th March and 21th September, at 5.58 am, a ray of sunlight would penetrate the sixty five metres between the entr-

118

ance and the shrine and bathes Amon-Ra and Ramses II in light. A few minutes later the ray would move on and fall on Harmakis. After about twenty minutes the light disappeared and it is really quite remarkable that the rays of light never struck Ptah, for Ptah is in fact the god of darkness.

The temple wall decorations celebrate the military grandeur of Ramses II. The poet Pentaur, serving at the court of the great Pharaoh, composed a long epic poem on the expedition of Ramses the Great in Syria. The poem, written in hieroglyphics, is engraved not only here at Abu Simbel, but also on the walls of other gigantic temples, such as those at Karnak and Luxor. During the long wars waged against the Hatti, a belligerent Syrian tribe which had formed alliances with several of the neighbouring populations, Pharaoh Ramses II gave his troops proof of rare martial valour. In the fifth year of his reign the Pharaoh, at the head of his army, advanced against the city of Atech or Quothshou, the ancient Emesus, to the northwest of Tripoli.

Betrayed by false refugees (Bedouin spies in the pay of the king of the Hatti), Pharaoh fell into an ambush and was suddenly surrounded by enemy troops. Ramses found himself alone with his personal guard, consisting of seventy-five war chariots, against an enemy possessing more than two thousand.

«Then» writes the poet Pentaur in exaltation of the glory of his lord, «extending his body to its full height, Pharaoh arrayed himself in the proud armour of the warrior. And whipping forward his chariot drawn by two horses, he flung himself into the fray. He was alone, completely alone, with no one beside him! His soldiers and his bodyguard watched from a distance as he leaped to the attack and defended himself like a hero. Two thousand five hundred chariots, each bearing three soldiers, surrounded him and crushed tight about him to cut him off. But he, undaunted, had with him neither princes nor generals nor soldiers!...».

In this moment of supreme danger, Ramses then addresses this fervent prayer to the supreme god of the pharaohs: «O thou, divine Amon, Lord of eternity, creator and organiser of the world, God who provides all, Lord of all the kingdoms of the earth... see, I am alone!... Are you not my father and I your son?... My arm has always done thy will. Have I not rendered you homage with my offerings? Remember the thirty thousand oxen sacrificed in your name and the temples of enormous blocks of granite I have raised to thee! Count the obeliscs I have erected in your honour! O divine Amon, now that I am alone and abandoned by all, I extend to you my hands and my prayer. Are you not stronger than a thousand archers, than thousands of heros?...».

Amon responds at last to Ramses' prayer:

«I am your father the sun, my right hand is with thee and, as you have said, I alone am worth more than millions of warriors! When I descend into the tumult of chariots which beseige you, you will see them fall and shatter like vases of clay under your horse's hooves!... I will turn to ice the hearts of your countless enemies, I will take the strength from their limbs, I will make fall the lances and quivers from their hands and I will fling them into the waters like crocodiles!... They will kill each other and cut each other's throats, and he who has fallen shall never rise again!...».

Then Ramses calls for help from the generals and horsemen who have not taken part in the battle: «Come forward», Pharaoh cries to them, «and tell me who among

◄ *The hawk-headed statue of Ra Harakht and a detail of the statue of Nefertari.*

The sanctuary with the statues of Harmakis, Ramses II as a divinity, Amon Ra and Ptah.

The pronaos with the eight Osirian pilasters.

you has sacrificed himself for his country more than I have done. While you sat tranquil in your camps, I went out alone against the enemy. Were it not for me, you would all be dead!...».

Evening falls and the poet lets us witness the outcome of the battle. Ramses' entire army, which had retreated, turns to advance again.

«They advanced over earth covered with corpses, all red with blood... Their feet found no place to rest, so many were the dead!...». When the battle is over, the generals acclaim Pharaoh and praise him for the victory: «O Ramses of the valiant heart, you have done alone more than a whole army could do. Before your victorious sword the land of the Hatti has bowed down!... Nothing can be compared to you when you fight for your people on the day of battle!... Impelled by the example of their leader, the Egyptian cavalry threw themselves into battle as the sparrow-hawk springs on its prey. The Pharaoh accomplished great of valour. All those who approached him fell beneath his blows. Soon the bodies of the enemy cut to pieces formed a mountain of bloody corpses...».

The role played by Ramses II in history comes to life in these epic pages. No wonder then that from Djebel Barkal to Narh el Keld (near Beirut), numerous stelae celebrate the deeds of this king to whom classic legend attributes victories similar to those of Thot-Mosis III, Seth I and Ramses III.

It is also a singular fact that Ramses II, in the continual glorification of himself, had a much smaller temple, barely ten metres long and dedicated to his wife Nefertari built beside his masterpiece. Never before in Egypt had the wife of a pharaoh been depicted on the façade of a temple, indeed only the wife of Ramses II ever did attain this honour.

For many long centuries the temples of Abu Simbel remained there, lapped by the waters of the Nile, perpetuating the memory, the greatness and the divinity of Ramses II. The danger that the temples might disappear beneath the waters of the artificial lake had world wide repercussions. UN-ESCO immediatley set up two commissions to study the problem of salvaging them. However finding a solution was not a simple matter both because of the structure of the temples and because of the material of which they are made. The final choice was a solution proposed by Sweden which involved complete removal of the

At left a representation of the goddess Isis (above) and the god Horus (below).

At right, Pharaoh immolates a group of prisoners.

overhanging rocky mass, the cutting up of the temples into pieces and their reconstruction on a plateau above the original level. First of all 17,000 holes were made in the stone through which resin was injected to consolidate the structure. Thirty three tonnes or resin and about the same weight of iron braces to prevent the stone from crumbling were found to be necessary.

As the waters of the Nile rose, and they rose much more rapidly than anticipated, the cutting and moving of the stones was started in a frantic race against time. The monuments were sawn into one thousand and thirty six blocks whose average weight was thirty tonnes to which must be added the eleven hundred and ten pieces cut from the surrounding rock.

The first block, bearing the number GA 1AO1, was removed on 21st May 1965. This was the start of the most fantastic enterprize involving the dismantling and reconstruction of a monument which archeologists had ever undertaken. The funerary complex of Ramses and Nefertari was reconstructed exactly as it had been on a site ninety metres above the original level. However it was soon realized that it was not possible to reconstruct the temple just like that because the weight of the artificial rock built above it would have caused the temple to crumble. Hence two enormous domes of reinforced concrete were built over it which were intered to take the pressure of the mountain and thus like an enormous bell-jar, to protect the sanctuary. The two

domes were then covered with the material which had been removed and the sand and the dust could be left to see to the filling of any gaps.

The removal of the temple from its original site was barely completed in time. By the end of the summer of 1965 the waters of the Nile slowly started to fill the now quite desolate caverns where the temples had once stood. Up above the big temple was complete again. All that was lacking to complete the picture was the «miracle of the sun» and this occurred punctually in February 1969. Then the light of the sun fell on the gods sitting in the shrine just as it has done two thousand years previously. Ramses II and his architectural masterpiece continued to exist in spite of everything.

The facade of the ''Small'' Temple or Temple of Hathor dedicated to Nefertari.

The jagged rocky coast bathed by the waters of the Red Sea at Sharm el Sheikh.

Monastery of Saint Catherine; a detail of the basilica of ► the Transfiguration and the mount of Moses.

THE SINAI PENINSULA

About twenty million years ago, Egypt, Sinai and the Arab peninsula were united in a single block. Then, huge terrestrial devastations led to the separation of the lands, and the southern Sinai peninsula remained isolated, giving rise to two large gulfs: to the west, the Gulf of Suez, whose maximum depth is barely 95 metres, and the Gulf of Aqaba to the east, which instead reaches a depth of 1,800 metres. The latter gulf is a part of the big land fissure — called Rift — which extends from the chain of Taurus as far as Kenya. The great sismic activity of the past and the tremendous eruptive phenomena have given Sinai its characteristic imprint. The most important peaks are the Gebel Musa (Moses' mountain, 2285 metres) and Mount St Catherine (Gebel Kathrina, 2642 metres), the highest on the peninsula.

The west coast, then, that from Sharm el Sheikh to Ras Mohammed goes as far as Taba, is distinguished by numerous coral reefs that occur in succession, one after the other.

MONASTERY OF ST CATHERINE

The smallest diocesis in the world is at the same time the oldest Christian monastery still in existence in the world and houses also the richest collection of icons and precious manuscripts.

We can find the first news regarding the Monastery of St Catherine in the chronicles of the Patriarch of Alexandria, Eutychios, who lived during the 9th century: said chronicles tell us how Helena, the mother of Emperor Constantine, remained so impressed by the sacredness of these places that in the year 330 she ordered the construction of a small chapel on the site where the burning bush had been located. The chapel was dedicated to the Blessed Virgin Mary.

Emperor Justinian in 530 ordered the construction of a much larger basilica: the one which would be the Church of the Transfiguration. It was then that the monastery took on the appearance of a massive fortification which characterizes it even today.

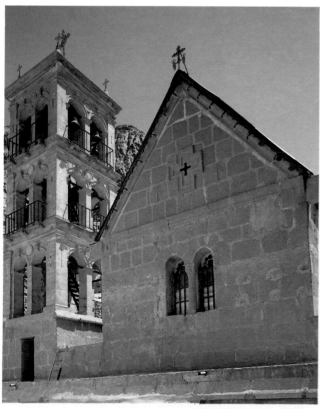

INDEX

© Copyright by CASA EDITRICE BONECHI, Via Cairoli 18/b - 50131 Florence - Italy
Tel.55/576841 - Fax 55/5000766
E-mail: bonechi@bonechi.it - Internet: www.bonechi.it

*Printed in Italy by Centro Stampa Editoriale Bonechi.
Photographs from the Archives of Casa Editrice Bonechi taken by
M. Carpiceci; L. Di Giovine; P. Giambone.*

ISBN 88-8029-035-5

* * *

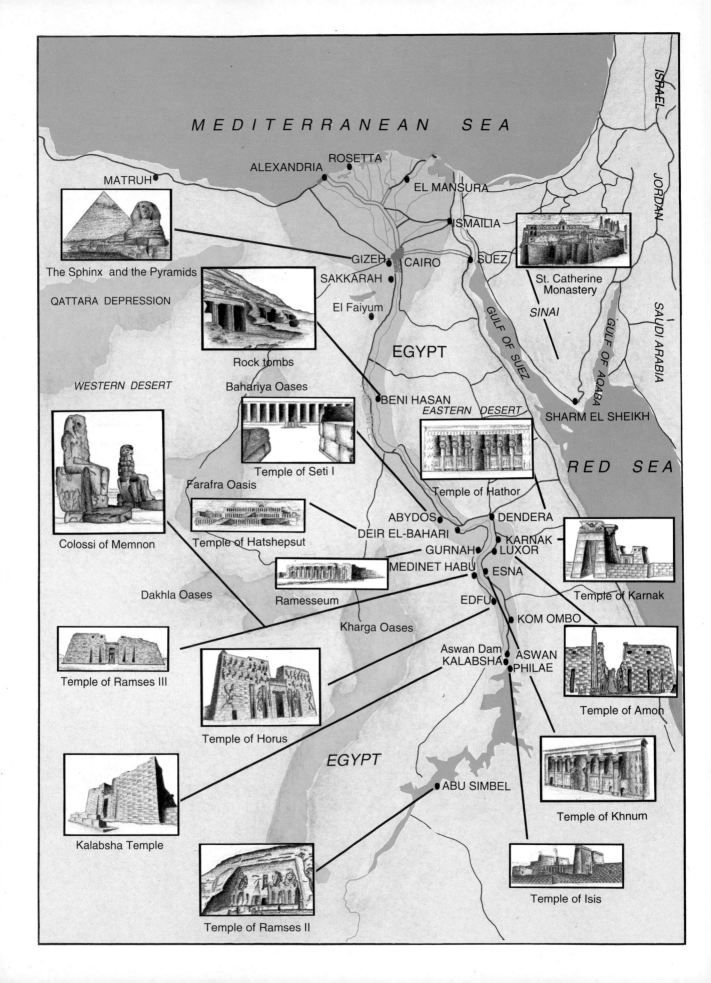

MEDITERRANEAN SEA

ISRAEL

JORDAN

ROSETTA

ALEXANDRIA

MATRUH

EL MANSURA

ISMAILIA

SUEZ

The Sphinx and the Pyramids

GIZEH · CAIRO

SAKKARAH

St. Catherine
Monastery

QATTARA DEPRESSION

El Faiyum

SINAI

SAUDI ARABIA

EGYPT

GULF OF SUEZ

GULF OF AQABA

Rock tombs

WESTERN DESERT

Barariya Oases

BENI HASAN

EASTERN DESERT

SHARM EL SHEIKH

RED SEA

Temple of Seti I

Colossi of Memnon

Farafra Oasis

Temple of Hathor

Temple of Hatshepsut

ABYDOS

DENDERA

DEIR EL-BAHARI

KARNAK

GURNAH

LUXOR

MEDINET HABU

ESNA

Dakhla Oases

Ramesseum

Kharga Oases

EDFU

Temple of Karnak

Temple of Ramses III

KOM OMBO

Aswan Dam
KALABSHA

ASWAN
PHILAE

Temple of Horus

Temple of Amon

Kalabsha Temple

ABU SIMBEL

EGYPT

Temple of Khnum

Temple of Isis

Temple of Ramses II